Prophecy

for

Profit

ABOUT THE AUTHORS

SASHA FENTON

 Sasha was born in Bushey, near Watford in Hertfordshire, England during the second world war. Her family are Jewish immigrants from Europe (mainly Poland) and many of them have had an interest in psychic or occult subjects. Most of them took their psychic or intuitive gifts for granted, as these were considered pretty normal among their peer group. Sasha became interested in palmistry in childhood, partly due to the fact that her mother knew something about it, although Sasha learned her craft initially from books and later by looking at hundreds of people's hands.

During her twenties, she read and learned all she could about astrology, and by the time of her Saturn return when she was around the age of 30, Sasha was earning a little pin money by writing up horoscopes for clients. She soon added Tarot reading to her list of skills. For several years in the 1980s, the only way she could make any money was through giving readings, but when she started earning money from her books, she gradually cut down the amount of time spent on her consultancy.

Despite working hard as a writer and now also as a publisher, Sasha still gives the occasional reading and she also run classes, lectures and workshops. Sasha is a past Secretary and President of the British Astrological and Psychic Society (BAPS), a past Chairman of the Advisory Panel on Astrological Education and a past member of the Executive Council of the Writers' Guild of Great Britain. Jan and Sasha started Zambezi Publishing in 1998 and they now plan to publish books written by a variety of skilled practitioners in the mind, body and spirit field.

Sasha has two children from her marriage to Tony Fenton, and a growing clan of grandchildren.

JAN BUDKOWSKI

 Jan's family were Catholic immigrants to Zambia from Poland, and Jan was actually born in a displaced persons' camp in Lusaka, Zambia during the second world war. His parents were refugees from the Nazi regime. Jan went to school in Lusaka and during his teens and twenties, in addition to doing all those sensible things such as getting a good education and going out to work, he spent eight years as lead guitar in a pop group, playing professionally at dances and other "gigs" all around the country.

Jan has worked in the field of banking for 31 years, rising from a junior to a high executive position, and during this time he worked in Zambia, Zimbabwe and South Africa. Much of his work has been in the field of assessing and advising people about the financial realities associated with their small, medium and large businesses.

He has been interested in psychology, personal development and astrology for more years than he claims to remember. Before finally leaving South Africa in 1996, he handled the astrological research department of the Astrological Society of South Africa (ASSA).

He has written a book on the history and psychology of dreams with Sasha, is currently involved in developing the computer, design, database and website issues required by Zambezi Publishing, the business that he and Sasha started recently.

Jan has one son, Mitchell, who is happily doing his own thing in Cape Town, South Africa.

In their spare time (?), Sasha and Jan enjoy fly-fishing, travelling, reading, fly-fishing and occasionally a bit of fly-fishing as well...

Prophecy for Profit

*The Essential Career and Business Guide
for those who give Readings*

**Sasha Fenton
and
Jan Budkowski**

ZAMBEZI PUBLISHING

First published in Great Britain in 1999
by Zambezi Publishing
P.O. Box 188 Brentford
Middlesex TW8 8RW
Fax: +44 (0)181 568-4992
Find us on the Internet at:
http://www.zampub.com
e-mail: zambezi@compuserve.com or
info@zampub.com

British Library Cataloguing-in-Publication Data:
A catalogue record for this book is available from the British Library.

ISBN 0-9533478-1-8

Edited by Jan Budkowski
Typeset by Zambezi Publishing
Cover design by Jan Budkowski © 1999
Printed and bound in Great Britain by:
Antony Rowe Ltd,
Bumper's Farm, Chippenham, Wiltshire
1 3 5 7 9 8 6 4 2

Contents

When "Spirit" is important and money isn't - if you need
to earn a living - materialism - marketing - a day's work
for a day's pay -what any successful business person
will tell you - what any professional psychic will tell
you

What qualifications do you need - beginners section -
early days as a professional consultant - where to find
training - training in astrology - training for healing -
other divinations - watching the professionals - books
& other literature - groups & organisations

Do you need training - an astrologer's view - special
advice - advice-giving

Part-time consulting - should you keep your consultancy
a secret

Location, location, location - accessibility - a place to
work in - your own appearance - a few essentials - food

& drink - smoking - drinking - your loo - clients with children - your waiting area - insurance and other protection - the loneliness of the long-distance Reader

ing - dozy clients - foreign clients - clients from hell - it's not over until the fat lady sings - the oversized bosom syndrome - bad news - Veronica - a plate of jelly - can I have the good stuff now, please? - the proof of the pudding - what can be expected from a reading - overdemanding clients - the Royal Marine Bandsman syndrome

Dedications

We dedicate this book to Jan's mother Helena Budkowska,
and our friends, William Grey Campbell and Barbara Ellen.

Acknowledgements

We gratefully acknowledge the following old and new friends
for the ideas and advice that they have given us,
both in recent months and over many years.
These have all been put to good use in this book.
So, we extend a hearty "thank you" to:

Jonathan Dee, Tracey Risman, Robert Currey,
Barbara Ellen, Sheila McGuirk, Dave and Eve Bingham,
Molly Ann Fairley, Betty Nugent, Roy Gillett,
Sue Lilley, Malcolm Wright, Matthew Turnell (of Barclays
Bank), Adam Fronteras (of BAPS)
and to the many Readers, clients and guinea-pigs
who have contributed to our book.
And last but definitely not least,
to our accountant, Howard Markham, for his
invaluable financial and taxation advice.

HOW YOU CAN HELP US TO HELP OTHERS

We would like to mention that there are two ways in which you can help us to produce the kind of material that we can pass on to others in the future.

The first is to write in, fax or e-mail us with any comments, helpful tips or additions that you would like us to put in future editions of this book. We won't be able to respond to your letters, but we will take any really good ideas on board and include them when revising this book. If you want your name to be acknowledged, please let us know; if you wish to remain anonymous, you may do so.

A second way in which you can help us is to take a look at the questionnaire that appears in the back of this book. The questionnaire is designed to help us formulate our next book in this series, which will be directed towards those who work in the fields of alternate and complementary medicine, therapies, beauty treatments and so on. The questionnaire will help us to understand more fully the problems and joys of these particular forms of employment while we put together the various issues to be covered in the book. By the way, we intend to call our new book **"An Alternative Income"**, and we hope to be able to publish it later this year (1999).

Should you wish to be placed on a mailing list for our next book and any others, please complete and send us the mailing list form, also included at the end of this book (or e-mail us with all the details listed in the form). Our address is c/o Zambezi Publishing, and the full address is listed in the appendix at the back of this book.

Any substantiated information that applies in your own country would be of interest to us, for future editions of this book. We would welcome such details, which should be sent to Zambezi Publishing at the address/e-mail address shown in the appendix.

DISCLAIMER

When British people read the following disclaimer, they will think we have gone completely off our heads, but those in the USA will understand our reasons, and this book will be released in the States, as well as other countries around the world.

The British legal system makes it difficult for anyone to make money out of frivolous law suits - even if they could find a solicitor daft enough to take such a thing on. In the USA things are different, so we have taken the advice of Dan Poynter, who has written an excellent book on publishing (The Self-publishing Manual), by taking up his offer of adapting his disclaimer for our own use. If you read through the disclaimer, it contains quite a number of comments and facts that are appropriate to our work. So here - with thanks to Mr. Poynter - is the disclaimer:

Warning - Disclaimer

This book is designed to provide information in regard to the subject matter covered. It is sold with the understanding that the publisher and authors are not engaged in rendering legal, accounting or other professional services. If legal or other expert assistance is required, the services of a competent professional should be sought. The reader's individual circumstances may require customised solutions for specific issues.

It is not the purpose of this manual to reprint all the information that is available to the authors and/or publisher, but to complement, amplify and supplement other texts. You are urged to read all the available material, learn as much as possible about consultancy work and to tailor the information to your individual needs.

Consultancy work is not a get-rich-quick scheme. Anyone who decides to run a consultancy must expect to invest a lot of time and effort. For many people, such work is a rewarding business on a number of different levels.

Every effort has been made to make this manual as complete and as accurate as possible. However, there may be mistakes, both typographical and in content. Therefore, this text should be used only as a general guide and not as the ultimate source of consultancy information. Furthermore, this manual contains information only up to the printing date.

The purpose of this manual is to educate and entertain. The authors and Zambezi Publishing shall have neither liability nor responsibility to any person or entity with respect to any loss or damage caused, or alleged to be caused, directly or indirectly by the information contained in this book.

If you do not wish to be bound by the above, you may return this book to the publisher for a full refund.

Two amusing ideas emerge from the above disclaimer, the first being that if you really do wish to return the book due to desiring not to be bound by the disclaimer, please do so immediately and please pack it so that it arrives back here in a state where it can be sold on to another purchaser. Zambezi Publishing will not refund anything for an obviously well-read, damaged or dog-eared book.

Secondly, we love the phrase "neither reliability nor responsibility to any person or entity", because in our kind of business, it is just possible that an "entity" could become miffed with us, and we would hate to find ourselves under a psychic attack from the other side!

A SECOND DISCLAIMER

While researching this book we heard an unsubstantiated story about a Reader who was badly ripped off by a member of the public. Whether true or not, it may be useful and even necessary for Readers to consider issuing disclaimers to members of the public. We are sure that this is already the case in the USA, where frivolous lawsuits are not that unusual. We suggest that if you feel the need to issue a disclaimer, you take proper legal advice before doing so. In the meantime, the wording on the following sample Readers' disclaimer might help. You are welcome to use it, and you can print it on a slip of paper that is given to each client.

Sample Readers' disclaimer

Those of us who work as Readers try to give as much accuracy in our readings as is possible, but ours is not an exact science. Often we are only given shadows from which we interpret our client's lives and futures as best we can. If you need exact accuracy from a reading, or for the wording to exactly describe what is to happen in your future, please do not even think of having a reading today or on any other day. If you are happy to be bound by the fact that any reading that I give you may be a little vague or off-centre in some areas, or that I may use words that are inexact, please accept that your decision to have a reading constitutes a verbal contract by which you agree to be bound. If you don't wish to be bound by this verbal contract, please do not request a reading here.

Code of Ethics

While the disclaimer might be amusing to our British readers, a Code of Ethics is a serious matter for any consultant. Read and use the following sample as your own benchmark for the high standards of your work:

It shall be the aim of every Reader to provide a service that reflects both the professional and spiritual integrity of our profession.

By your own example, encourage all with whom you come into contact to develop an awareness and understanding of our subject(s) and the spiritual reality that they represent.

Any consultant who accepts work at any festival or other official function should do so under the conditions of that festival in respect of the type of work, the behaviour of the consultant and the agreed structure of the fees thereof. (If a fee structure or part-payment structure is applicable.)

At all times a consultant shall conduct him/herself in a manner befitting a professional and in no way should they bring the good name of our work into disrepute.

Some societies ask their members not to write columns in newspapers about Royal personages, politicians or celebrities without specific permission, but we think that this idea is unworkable. However, it is unethical to suggest that such a celebrity is likely to be ill, to suffer badly in their future life or even to die at a specified date or a specific manner - especially if the offending article is written purely for the titillation of the public and for monetary gain.

It is also very unethical to suggest to a client that something nasty is about to befall him or a member of his family, and that this can be averted by paying the consultant a large (or even a small) fee to bless candles or to perform some kind of clearance in order to handle or divert this. If a client asks for such a service to be done, that is a different matter, and an appropriate service and price can then be arranged between the consultant and the client. Finally, no magic, ritual or any other kind of practice should be done against another person or entity, as such a "black" act will not only rebound on the client but it will also rebound upon the Reader.

In short, be ethical, look after your own spirituality and look after your career, and these will then look after you in return.

INTRODUCTION

This book is designed for Readers who wish to take a professional approach to their work. It is not a treatise on how to extract large sums of money from people who are suffering or who need answers to problems. Indeed, it doesn't matter if you are the kind of Reader who wants to give a service without asking for payment in exchange. This book is simply designed to help you to organise your work and your life in an efficient and cost-effective manner. Those of you reading this book who want to make a part or full-time living out of the business of running a consultancy, or who want to improve a currently successful consultancy, will find much beneficial advice in our book. This book obviously has much to offer the beginner, but it will fill in gaps and offer ideas and suggestions to even the most experienced Reader.

Jan Budkowski's 31 years in banking involved him in advising people who started and ran businesses of all sizes and types. Sasha's 25 years as a professional consultant have taken her all over the world and into all the different kinds of situation that any Reader is likely to meet. Many other people have contributed ideas to this book, and their comments and stories appear throughout it. Some of the stories that enliven our book offer salutary warnings, others offer useful tips, and some tales are hilarious accounts of the kind of things that are all in a day's work for the average Reader. This should help you to realise that the problems, experiences and the pleasures that you obtain from your job are universal, and that you are not alone.

The divination explosion

From the very dawn of history, in every country in the world, in every culture that has ever existed, and at every point in time, there have been people from every walk of life who have consulted seers.

In western society over the past couple of hundred years or so, our business was considered somewhat occult and not something that people spoke about openly. During Sasha's early days as a professional consultant, many clients made their appointments under false names, and it was often impossible to ask a client for a phone number in case an appointment needed to be moved. People didn't want their partners or their colleagues to know that they were visiting an astrologer or palmist, in case they were thought peculiar. Sasha used to joke that some of her customers came to her wrapped in a brown paper bag. Nowadays, everybody and his dog visits clairvoyants, astrologers, Rune readers, Feng Shui experts and so on. Mainstream television programmes cover these subjects, and these days many ordinary people have a goodly amount of knowledge about our arts and crafts. At last the mystery has gone - and a good job too! Some say that the decline of organised religion is responsible for the popularity of our work, but we don't believe that, because people of every variety of eastern and western religious belief consult Readers. It is more likely that counselling of all kinds - be it psychic, holistic, astrological, health-related or psychotherapeutic - has become the norm, and a more relaxed attitude to seeking outside advice is now in effect. As part of this pattern, readings have climbed out of the closet, and there is now an explosion in the number of people who are taking up this work.

The benefits of running a consultancy

The benefits of running a Reader's consultancy are many and varied. A consultancy offers self-employment to those who have had enough of working for an employer, a bridge while looking for a new job, a replacement income for those who have been made redundant, or a creative outlet for mothers of small children who can only devote a couple of hours a week to the task. It can suit those who need to work from home and those who want to travel the world and earn money while on the move.

There is a "feel-good" factor in helping others, and to giving a good service to those who need it, and there is also an inner satisfaction to be derived from working in a spiritual manner. Our work has room for those who are mystical, practical, artistic, down to earth, academic, earthy, ordinary and extraordinary. There is room for every type of Reader in every discipline, and there are clients with a plethora of different needs out there to be taken care of.

So for those of you who are contemplating taking up this work, and for those of you who are already active in the field, read on to discover how to handle your work in a businesslike way. Discover how to minimise your expenses and losses, and to maximise your gains... without losing your ethics, your integrity, your spirituality - or your clients.

Chapter 1

PROFESSIONAL CONSULTING

Who is this book for?

When "Spirit" is important and money isn't – if you need to earn a living – materialism – marketing – a day's work for a day's pay –what any successful business person will tell you – what any professional psychic will tell you

In this book we use the word Reader with a capital "R" as a title for those who give readings. We refer to various Readers and their clients as "he" or "she" depending upon what seems most appropriate to the topic at the time. We are equal opportunity writers!

When "Spirit" is important and money isn't

Your motivation for giving readings may primarily be spiritual and you may have no need to earn money from your work, and you may even feel that it is wrong for you to do so. If this is the case, you will still find plenty in this book to show you how to make a success of what you do and to minimise the aggravation factor. If you need opportunities to give your work for little or nothing, consider offering your services to your local Spiritualist Church. You will have all the pleasure of helping people who need a reading, you can raise money for charity and at the same time become part of our wonderful spiritual world, without having to sully your conscience with filthy lucre. There is absolutely nothing wrong with this attitude, and we in this book are under no circumstances interested in pressurising you into changing your outlook.

If you need to earn a living

If you need to earn good money, you can easily do so without ripping off the public. We will show you how to give your clients a quality service while at the same time enjoying a comfortable lifestyle from the fruits of your efforts.

Our book is for the most part a business book and it contains much that is similar to the kind of information that you will find in regular business books, but you will find the explanations in our book far easier to read and to understand than in the average business book.

The chances are that if you are a crystal gazer or a sand Reader, you won't have read the usual business books that concentrate on such matters as finance, bookkeeping, cashflow, business plans and so on, and you may never have read a book on marketing either. Although this book has sections on all these subjects and much more, it concentrates strictly on how to apply these concepts to the business of being a Reader. So if you want to maximise your profits and minimise your losses without losing your soul, read on...

You will have already noticed and you will see again and again in this book that there must be a spiritual element to all that you do, but there is no reason for you to starve for the sake of "upstairs". You can make a good living - perhaps not a magnificent one, but a good enough living, if you set about your work in the right way.

Materialism

Whilst writing this book, the topic of materialism has come up in conversation with others on several occasions. Many of those who are new to spiritual work (and some who are not so new) have the perception that it is wrong to have more than the bare minimum that is needed for survival. Apparently it is spiritually incorrect to want money and possessions, and it is wrong to take a commercial view of our work - or indeed any other kind of work. This anti-materialistic view was not always prevalent among psychics, it came about after the explosion of interest in Indian and Asian religious concepts that swept westwards on the heels of the Beatles' friend, the Maharishi Mahesh Yogi in the 1970s.

Oriental and Eastern peoples, whether they come from India, Hong Kong, Malaya or Saudi Arabia, are often extremely money-minded. Wives drive their husbands crazy to give them the kind of homes and goods that will give them "face" and thus make them the envy of the neighbourhood. Men will work themselves to death in order to obtain status symbols, and worse still, dubious business practices are often the order of the day. The religious folk from these countries fight hard against this tide of crass materialism. They take the opposite road of living an extremely simple life and of preaching that the Almighty will provide their followers with sufficient for their survival.

The chances are that those who are reading this book will have been brought up in one of the Judeo-Christian western societies. These have always emphasised the need for charity, fair play, decency in business dealings and in not looking too rich or too flash. We don't need to have anti-materialism drummed into us; on the contrary, spiritual people need to know that there is nothing wrong in having "abundance" as long as it is obtained by fair means.

If you want confirmation of where all this is coming from, take a look at your television next time there is a human tragedy, and see how many oil-rich or trade-rich eastern peoples rush in to help. It will be Christian Aid, Oxfam, Medicine Sans Frontiers and even the Israelis most likely!

The average western Tarot Reader doesn't need lessons in anti-materialism...

Marketing

In any business, whether it be manufacturing, selling goods or giving a service, you have to bring your "product" to the notice of the public. Marketing is the key to building a clientele and in this book we will show you how to go about this. Sitting at home waiting for business to walk through the door all by itself won't get you anywhere. We have all come across the kind of female clients who would, "love to meet a nice man" but who do nothing to make this happen. We are sure that you, like us, have pointed out to these lonely ladies that sitting night after night in front of the television isn't going to do anything to make their dreams come true. It would be terrific if the right kind of man or the right kind of income jumped out of the television screen and landed in our laps, but it doesn't, so whether it is love or business that is wanted, marketing is the key.

Do a day's work for a day's pay

It may sound simplistic for us to say this, but if you want to earn money you must be prepared to work for it. Being self-employed requires far more self-motivation than going out to work. If you work in a proper job, you will doubtless be under the eagle eye of supervisors, managers and directors who keep your nose to the grindstone. You may have targets to meet and budgets to work within, and if you don't do so you will soon find yourself out of a job. Working people must offer their employers their best efforts or they are not worth employing. If you are self-employed you must become your own supervisor, manager and slave-driver or you won't succeed.

We all know Readers who stop work the moment that they go down with a slight cold, putting their clients off for weeks or even months. When they begin to feel in the mood to make the effort once more, they are surprised and aggrieved to discover that their clientele has disappeared off the face of the earth. If you only want to work for a few hours each week that is fair enough, but if you want to make money, you will have to do at least the same hours that you would expect to do in a normal job. If you charge the kind of fees that we recommend in this book and if you work at least a forty hour week, you will make a living. Of course, you will have to build your clientele first, but we will show you how to do this. You may not devote every one of your forty hours to readings, because marketing, client building, broadcasting, travelling and administration can all be counted as part of the job, but the more time you can put into seeing clients, the more money you will earn.

Sitting around and watching the soaps on daytime television brings some people inordinate pleasure, but the only people who earn money out of the soaps are the actors, writers, producers, studio staff and marketers who sell the programmes. Earn your living first and if you must follow a favourite soap, record it and watch it after your day's work is done.

What any successful business person will tell you

Be enthusiastic about your work, be pushy, make it happen, keep your eyes on the stars of success, fame, glory, having money to spare after paying your bills or anything else that you want, and it will happen. Ensure that you have a good "product" and market it well, keep working and build for the future, save some of your money for the quiet times and keep cheerful, and you will be a winner.

What any professional psychic will tell you

Keep a positive mental attitude and even your own Spiritual guides will become excited by your progress. If you are negative, lazy, uninspired or boring, they will find someone else to channel their love and inspiration through.

SKILLS AND QUALIFICATIONS

What qualifications do you need – beginners section – early days as a professional consultant – where to find training – training in astrology – training for healing – other divinations – watching the professionals – books & other literature – groups & organisations

What qualifications do you need?

Generally, no qualifications whatsoever are required for anyone who wishes to work as a professional Reader. The vast majority of Consultants have absolutely no qualifications at all, and the chances are that nobody ever asks them to display any. If you decide to teach in a formal institution such as the UK adult education services, you will definitely need some kind of accreditation. If you want your name to be advertised in a register belonging to a particular organisation, you will need to be vetted by that organisation. If you want to work on a particular organisation's stand at a psychic and mystics festival, you will need to be accepted as part of that organisation and to abide by its rules. The fact is that, for most Readers, the only qualification that is needed is the ability to do the job.

If you are a beginner you will be avid for information on ways of increasing your skills, and you may be keen to look into the possibilities of obtaining qualifications. If you have been working for some years, you may still wish to improve your skills or qualifications in your own divination, or you may wish to add a new divination to your pantheon. Despite some of the scare stories that are being put about in the UK about European Union regulations, you don't need any qualifications at all to work as a Reader. When we made enquiries about this several years ago, we were told that nothing was needed and that this situation was unlikely to change. It is, nevertheless, a good idea to keep abreast of developments, as one never knows when political expediency may alter systems previously cast in stone. The situation regarding Therapists is a different matter, as anybody who treats patients must be registered with a relevant organisation and they must be properly qualified and certified. This is the case in most western countries and not just the UK.

Beginners section

If you are a beginner, one of two scenarios will apply, in that you will either feel very unsure of your abilities or you may be overconfident. Fortunately, the first of these two scenarios is far more common. If you feel uncertain, don't stop working but look around for skill-building opportunities. If you are overconfident, you will soon fall flat on your face - at which point you will either give up the job for good or decide that you could do with a bit more information and training.

If you are an absolute beginner, you will find that one of the best ways of gaining experience is by doing the job! This is a catch-22 situation, in that you can't do the job without experience and you can't obtain experience without doing the job! The way around this is to give free readings to as many people as you can reach, and you will find no shortage of volunteer guinea-pigs! Tell your neighbours and ask them to tell their friends that you are happy to give them a free reading, and do the same for your colleagues at work. Try to see as many strangers as you can because this will help you to develop your skills much faster than if you simply confine yourself to those whose circumstances are familiar to you. When you start to find yourself being recommended to others you will be ready to "go professional". If you are still unsure of yourself, charge only a small fee and only increase it to a reasonable amount when your confidence has grown.

Sasha's stories:
Early days as a professional Consultant

In my own case, I was so ignorant about this business that it didn't occur to me to charge for the palmistry readings that I occasionally gave, until in 1974 I met an astrologer who was charging a small fee. At that time my astrology abilities were growing apace and beginning to match my considerable knowledge of hand reading. My children were small and not in particularly good health, which meant that going out to work was difficult for me. I began to look into the possibility of charging, and right from the start I managed to find the number of clients that I felt I could reasonably handle.

Where to find training for Spiritual work

If you are keen on anything of a psychic or mediumistic nature, your starting point is your local Spiritualist Church or centre. There you will find courses of training and development circles that you can join. The centre members should be able to point you in the direction of the main national Spiritualist organisations that operate in your country. You will find books, literature and people to chat to, and you will soon find yourself visiting other centres in your area, to see the best visiting mediums and to watch them work.

Training in astrology

Astrologers tend to be the most literate (even verbose) of all the groups, and there are many opportunities for all kinds of courses. Obviously if you live in a city it is easier to get to actual classes than if you are stuck out in the wild, but there are plenty of excellent postal courses on offer that can link you with a personal tutor. In London in the UK, there are all kinds of courses, from one-day workshops, six-week introductory sessions, three-year diplomas and every other kind of course or workshop that you can think of. All the major schools offer certificates and diplomas for those who complete their courses. Some set examinations but others will be satisfied if you simply complete the course successfully.

The Urania Trust (their name may change during 1999 but the address will remain the same) in Great Britain publishes a truly wonderful directory that contains everything you could possibly need to know about where to find anything related to astrology. The information in this book is not confined to the UK scene, it is international. At the time of writing, this costs £5 in the UK. Details about this terrific reference book and much else can be found in the appendix at the back of this book. Don't forget to try the Internet for information, as this is crammed with astrology data.

Training for healing

Although healing doesn't fully come into the realm of this book (apart from the general considerations and some of the financial chapters), many Consultants are keen to learn this craft. These days the buzz-word is Reiki Healing, and there seem to be Reiki courses available all over the place. The Federation of Spiritual Healers offers training and there are other reputable organisations around in the UK and elsewhere. Therapists should buy magazines and publications that cover their particular interests, because these advertise people, groups and organisations who offer training in many different kinds of therapy. Your local Spiritualist centre or Church will also have information on tuition for healing.

Other divinations

Oddly enough, it is hard to find training in Palmistry, so if you want to read hands you will have to fall back on books, unless you can find a palmist in your area who is willing to give you training. The only site we found on the Internet is The Palmistry Center in Quebec, but possibly they may be able to put you in touch with teaching organisations in other parts of the world. There once used to be a UK society for palmists, but this now appears to be defunct. Graphologists definitely do have organisations to turn to. Magazines in the mind, body and spirit field, and the Internet, are probably your best starting point for looking up these organisations. If you want to read the Runes, scan a crystal ball, read sand or coffee-grounds, either look out for books on your subject or search the wonderful, wonderful Internet. If you aren't into computing, you may well have a friend who can help you out with this.

Watching the professionals

Whatever your speciality, make a point of going to psychic fairs and festivals. Depending upon the size and scope of the festival, you will be able to pick up leaflets advertising products, information on courses, local Readers and much more. While you are there, treat yourself to a reading or two in order to see how others in your field go about things.

Attend meetings, lectures, demonstrations or group events in your line of work. Pick up any magazines, newsletters and literature that you see lying around and join any organisation that looks interesting. Write to the letters page of any publication that appears to be allied to your own interests, because someone may be kind enough to reply to your request for tuition or information. This is even more likely if you make it clear that you are prepared to pay for tuition. It isn't that Readers are materialistic or selfish, it is just that we are always being asked to teach or hand out information for nothing, and we just can't spare the time for it. We have to earn a living just like anyone else.

Books and other literature

Interesting books can be found in the oddest places. Perhaps there is a shop in your area that sells mind, body and spirit material? Try normal book shops, your local library and scour second hand book shops, and even the thrift and charity shops for nuggets of gold. It is worth asking a second-hand book dealer to look out for mind, body and spirit books that come his way, and to ring you when new items come into stock. If you borrow books from friends, please be scrupulous in returning them.

If a friend or a colleague has a book that interests you, rather than borrowing it, take a note of the author, title, publisher and ISBN number, and try ordering the book through your local book shop, the Internet, or order it directly from the publishers. Whilst doing so, it is useful to ask if the author has written anything else in that line. All publishers produce catalogues of new books once or twice a year, and some will send you a catalogue of all their books in the mind, body and spirit range. Most authors keep stocks of their own books and if you locate the author through his publisher, you can find out what else he has to offer. This is sometimes the only way of finding a book that is out of print. Bear in mind that publishing wheels can grind exceedingly slowly, so don't expect a quick response. If you write to us here at Zambezi Publishing, we will send you our own small book list and also details of our forthcoming titles. (Don't forget to print your address very clearly and to give us a contact telephone number).

Look through the magazines that are relevant to your skills to see if there is a mail-order house that supplies books and literature. If anyone is offering to sell back numbers of your favourite magazine or any old books, buy them.

Bear in mind that not all those who write books are brilliant, and some magazine articles are real dross, so don't swallow the words of a single author wholesale. Read as great a spread of writers as you can and allow your common sense and intuition to guide you as to what is worth taking on board and what isn't.

Groups and organisations

Groups and organisations send out newsletters that will keep you abreast of current events and current thinking, and some arrange regular get-togethers that allow you to network with others in your line of work. There may be a help line that you can call if you have a real problem. Simply belonging to such an organisation can give you credibility if you decide to promote yourself in the media. If you are the type of person who enjoys being part of a Committee, offer to join one. The chances are that the organisation will be delighted to hear from you, and becoming involved in any organisation from the inside will teach you a great deal about the business end of your job. (Such an experience will also teach you a great deal about fragile egos!) Often, simply joining an organisation and reading its publication makes you feel less alone, and it will help you to network with others in your line of work.

You may join a group or organisation only to find that the people in it appear to be stand-offish, unfriendly and unwelcoming. Don't immediately turn around and give up on the group, give it a bit of time. Often it just takes a little time before you become known and accepted. What should happen in all such organisations is that the committee members should make a point of personally welcoming new members when they appear at meetings or conferences, and of introducing them to older members. Such older members should then be asked to take a newcomer under their wing and befriend them until they have found their feet. Unfortunately, this kind of man-management rarely happens, newcomers are left floundering, and the upshot is that many newcomers back off and leave the organisation. This is a shame, as all such organisations spend committee meetings agonising on how to find ways of increasing their membership, completely missing the fact that they can lose new members very quickly if they don't make them feel welcome. Networking is useful for everybody, and there is no guarantee that just because someone is an established member of some organisation or other that they have nothing to learn from someone who is new to the organisation, while the newcomer can obviously learn something from the old hands.

DO YOU NEED COUNSELLING SKILLS?

Do you need training - an astrologer's view - special advice - advice-giving

"A great profession has grown up around counselling, but who listens to counsellors anyway?"
(James Whale, radio and television presenter and journalist)

Do you need training to be a counsellor?

Telling other people how to live is a very enjoyable pastime, but is this counselling? If you truly see yourself as a counsellor, do first take some training, but before you plunge ahead and book yourself onto a course, look around to see what is available. Check to see what such courses cover. Look into the time scale that the course will take, see exactly what kind of studying or work will be required of you, and most importantly, take note of the fees and charges. Find out what you will be qualified for when you have completed the course. When you think you have found the right course, ask if you can be put in touch with one or two people who have already completed it. If there is any hesitation over this, give the organisation second thoughts. If you can speak to a past student, ask them what they have got out of their course and whether they think it is good value.

If you don't intend to get into serious counselling, you don't need any training at all, but one thing you can do is to learn to listen, and by this we mean really listen. Very few people have the first idea of how to listen without immediately jumping in with their two-pennyworth of opinion and advice. For so many clients, simply being able to talk to a sympathetic outsider who shuts up and listens in a friendly manner, gives them more spiritual and mental healing than anything else on earth.

Please bear in mind that you cannot put someone's life right in an hour or two. If a client consults a good counsellor or even a psychotherapist, this will involve a number of appointments taken over period of time with exercises, homework and perhaps group therapy as part of the package. You can't be expected to obtain the same results in a one-off reading. Sometimes all you can do is to open your client's mind to fresh ways of thinking about themselves and their predicament, and maybe go on to suggest that they seek out a qualified counsellor for further help. If you know someone who you think can help your client and who is happy for their name and phone number to be given out, pass these details on.

An astrologer's view

we remember some years ago coming across a very interesting article in an American astrology magazine written by a man who was obviously a sensitive and intelligent astrologer. He said that he had clients on his books who had been in therapy for months or even years at considerable expense to themselves. He cited one case where it had taken the psychoanalyst over eighteen months simply to work out what was the matter with his client! An astrologer must be able to do this within the first half-hour of the reading and also to come up with all the right answers during the course of the reading - and all for a minuscule fraction of the amount of money that a psychoanalyst can expect to earn. This is not to malign the name of psychoanalysis, because not every psychoanalyst takes eighteen months to work out what his client's problem is. Sometimes the kind of time-consuming techniques that therapists and analysts use are just what the client needs. Sometimes a twelve-step programme with Alcoholics Anonymous or some other such organisation is required. However, this just goes to show what the general public expect of us and also the high standards that we may expect of ourselves.

Sometimes it is a stray comment that comes out during a reading that can turn a client's life around. We remember the case of a friend who was married and at the same time also involved in a long-term affair with her boss. The clairvoyant who she consulted picked all this up and told her that she was dealing with two incredibly selfish men who were happy to bully her and to use her for their own ends. Our friend did leave her lover a year or so after the reading, and her husband some years after that. She is now happily living with someone who is good to her, and this future marriage was also picked up at that reading by the very perceptive clairvoyant.

Strictly speaking, the answer to the question of whether you need to give counselling as part of your job, is that you don't! This may surprise you, but it is a fact that as a Reader you don't have any obligation to counsel anybody about anything. Of course, many of you will be keen to help, advise and counsel your clients, but there are plenty of extremely successful Consultants who give absolutely no counselling whatsoever. They simply give the information that they have and then leave it to the client to work out what he or she is going to do about it all. By the same token, if you do develop counselling skills, then naturally you will be able to give a far more complete service to your clientele and thus be more competitive with your consultancy. There are also occasions when a client unexpectedly hits a low spot during a reading, and Jan and I feel that a certain basic level of counselling ability is really valuable. It is never a good idea to just let a client walk away in a low state of mind, especially if this may have been triggered by some revelation during the consultation.

Advice of a special nature

You will sometimes be faced by clients who have many problems that are outside your sphere of expertise. Such problems could be medical, legal, financial or some other matter that requires specialist knowledge. You can only give such a client the information that is at your disposal, and then only if you are very sure of what you are seeing. You can make fairly encouraging remarks if you think the client will come out on the right side of whatever pickle he is in, but you can't get involved in advice-giving in areas that are beyond you.

It is not up to you to give specific legal advice, you aren't qualified to do so. Much the same goes for medical matters. Some Readers are highly qualified in medical or therapeutic work and that is great for them, but if you don't come into this category you will need to take care. If you suspect that one of your clients is harbouring an illness, you must gently suggest that he or she seeks advice from a doctor, an alternative therapist or both. Don't take responsibility for technical topics that you don't understand. You can always advise a client to "take things easy for a while", and you may suggest that you don't think that a matter looks terribly serious, but you must always qualify such statements by suggesting that the cli-

---

Sasha's stories...

I have had clients who have expected me to sort out the most complicated of legal matters for them. One man in particular went on and on about some long-winded case, to the point where I decided that if I were a judge, I would definitely find for the other side! Another client who I will never forget had lost an absolute fortune as a result of having been a "Lloyd's Name". This is a special kind of investment that has made a great deal of money for those who put money into it in the past, but which in the late 1980s and early 1990s went the other way and incurred huge losses and expenses for its investors. My client was a Capricorn with strong Taurean qualities on his birthchart, so he found it hard to value himself as a person with just an ordinary amount of money in the bank. In short, this man needed the money for the survival of his ego. The poor man wanted me to provide him with sure-fire astrological stock-market advice so that he could win back all his lost riches. I gently pointed out to him that if I was able to do this, I would hardly be sitting in my back room giving readings for a living.

ent visit his doctor, "just to put his mind at rest". In short, in any dodgy situation, use your common sense and always cover your back.

We do the British lottery on occasion just for fun, and despite Sasha's much-vaunted clairvoyance, we have never yet won even the most basic prize on this. When asked in all seriousness if we can come up with a set of winning numbers, I point this out. I also state that this kind of luck or any other such mega changes of life are in the hands of providence and while we can often see an improvement coming, we can't make it happen.

Advice-giving

You may be totally dedicated to some kind of alternative medicine or therapy which you simply can't help recommending to your client. Before you scurry around your filing cabinet for just the right brochure or phone number, please bear in mind that most people prefer to find their own solutions to such matters. Your "grateful" client will very likely drop your lovingly given piece of information in the nearest trash can even before she arrives home. Having said all the foregoing, if your client appears to be sane or requests such information and there is some simple and practical advice that you have to offer, don't keep it to yourself, even if it is only to pass on the phone number of a decent local plumber!

Many Readers confuse counselling with advice-giving, and while many professional counsellors don't think much of advice-giving, it is a very natural human habit. Readers usually have experience and common sense and they find that a bit of practical advice will often help a mildly confused client. If the Reader is a medium who is channelling advice from a higher source, so much the better. (This comment comes from medium, Betty Nugent.).

Chapter 4

COMBINING CONSULTING WITH A "PROPER JOB"

Part-time consulting - should you keep your consultancy a secret

Part time consulting

"Don't give up your day job!" This is good advice to anybody who is starting out as an actor, singer, dancer, painter or writer, and it goes just as well for a budding Reader. If you have a "proper job" that you can tolerate and that brings in money, keep it. You may get to a stage where you can give up other types of work for good or you may not, depending upon your personal circumstances. You may be able to concentrate all your energies on your Consultancy business if you are married to a successful (and generous) partner, if you are retired with a good pension or if you have some other form of income and/or money behind you. However, if you are the main breadwinner, you will need to do something else until you can work up your business sufficiently to make a reliable living from it. Consultancy work isn't reliable, and there are times of the year when it disappears from the face of the earth, so having something else to turn to may well be essential. If you can make consulting the centre of your working life, there are other things that are allied to it that can boost your income. Such ancillary jobs can provide a welcome change of pace and they fill in the gaps when business is slow. We will look into some of the options in the next chapter. A good many really excellent Readers do have other careers, so if your job carries a good pension scheme or other perks, it would be silly to throw these away unless the job became completely intolerable.

Many people turn towards giving readings because nothing else works for them, while others are so desperate for money that anything that brings in a few pennies helps. Some work in the "black economy", drawing benefits from the government and earning cash on the side. This is illegal and it can lead to unexpected problems later on. As you will see when we look at things like tax, mortgages, social security and so on, it is far better to be "legitimate" if you want to succeed and to avoid problems. Some Readers have family setups that prevent them from having a "proper job", but they can manage to fit in a few readings to their lifestyle. The fact that this work can be done at home is often a great help in such situations.

There is no need to make a lifetime commitment to working as a Consultant. You may spend several years doing a day job and a few readings on the side, then perhaps go into consultancy work full time. You may then concentrate on something quite different for a few years and go back to running your consultancy on a part-time basis once again. You may combine readings with something that is artistic and creative, or with some other kind of self-employment. Jonathan Dee and Sasha have been writers and broadcasters for many years, but we still see the occasional client. If you have young children, you may be able to take turns with another mother, minding each other's children one day a week, while you both keep your hand in with part time occupations.

Should you keep your Consultancy secret?

With all that we say in this book about advertising, promoting your business and getting your name around, it may not be a great idea to talk too much about it in some other place of work, but you will have to be the best judge of this. If you work for a formal kind of organisation where you need to be taken seriously in a different light, it may be best to keep your interests quiet - let alone the fact that you actually give readings on a professional basis. Imagine trying to be taken seriously as a lawyer or banker if you start talking about ghost-busting, sand reading or clairvoyance?

The fact that you run a consultancy outside your normal hours may anger the people you work alongside, especially if they are struggling to make ends meet. You may have to put up with sniggering remarks and/or you may make your colleagues uneasy, especially if you ram what they consider to be strange beliefs down their throats. Some may become jealous of your success. On the other hand, your colleagues may be intrigued with what you do and interested to learn more; if you do a stint on the radio or television, they may be proud to be associated with a minor celebrity. Use your intuition and also some common sense about what you should or shouldn't reveal.

We cover the idea of giving readings in the workplace in another chapter, but it is worth remembering that bosses don't generally care for this kind of thing, and it may irritate your workmates. If a colleague asks quietly about your readings and then makes an arrangement to consult you away from your workplace, this should be fair enough, but touting for business around your workplace usually doesn't work. On the other hand, it may be perfectly acceptable. You will just have to work this out for yourself, taking into account your own circumstances.

A rather interesting twist on the theme of combining a day job and also drumming up business for a consultancy is unfolding in front of our eyes right now, while we are putting this book together. Our niece, Tracey, has entered the family business as an astrologer, Tarot reader and clairvoyant. To keep body and soul together while she is working her way up in her chosen career, she is doing a variety of other part-time jobs.

WORKING FROM HOME

Location, location, location – accessibility – a place to work in –
your own appearance – a few essentials – food & drink – smoking –
drinking – your loo – clients with children – your waiting area –
insurance and other protection – the loneliness of the long-distance Reader

The most obvious place for you to consider working in is your
home. The advantages are so evident that they almost hit you in the
face, but there can be disadvantages, as we shall see later. The list
below should outline most of the advantages pretty clearly.

- You are already on-site, so no rent or other fees are involved.
- You can use your own phone and answering machine.
- There are no travelling expenses and no time wasted by trav-
  elling.
- The venue is warm enough or cool enough to be comfortable.
- Your workroom can be arranged any way you want.
- Your computer, phone, files, crystal ball and so on are to hand.
- If anybody else touches or uses your stuff, it is only likely to
  be a member of your own family.
- You don't have to carry your goods or equipment anywhere.
- You can have a coffee and/or a snack when you feel like it.
- Family arrangements, such as picking up children from school
  etc. are easier to arrange.
- You can work the hours and the days that suit your lifestyle.

Location, location and location

Any real estate agent will tell you that the three most important issues to consider when buying a property are location, location and location, and this is definitely the case if you intend to see your clients in your own home. So before you go any further, take a look at the checklist below to see whether, on the face of things at least, your home has the right potential.

Is your home easy to get to by public transport?	__Y/N__
Is your home easy to find?	__Y/N__
Is your home in a reasonably pleasant location?	__Y/N__
Is there sufficient parking close by?	__Y/N__
Are your neighbours supportive?	__Y/N__
Do you have a suitable room that you can use?	__Y/N__
Is your home relatively easy to secure from thieves?	__Y/N__
Are you properly insured?	__Y/N__
Is your family setup suitable?	__Y/N__
Totals:	__Y/N__

The more "Yes" answers to the above questions, the better are your chances of working successfully from home.

Accessibility

Your first considerations should be the accessibility of your location. In plain English, this means that your clients should be able to reach you easily by public transport, and there should be sufficient parking for those who come by car. If your place is not easy to find, you will need to give very clear directions over the phone, or to Fax or post a map to your clients beforehand. It may be possible for you to enlist the help of a local shopkeeper to direct people to you. If you have a newsagent's shop that sells confectionery and cigarettes nearby that your clients can easily locate, you may be able to arrange for the shopkeeper to direct your clients to you. He may be happy to help if this brings custom into his shop. This is only really a viable option if you do less than two or three readings a week, otherwise the arrangement will put your shopkeeper to too much trouble.

Clients will be understandably nervous of visiting you if your venue is down a long, dark lane or if it is hidden in the depths of a downtrodden housing estate. Wherever you live, always ensure that your clients are clear about your address and the number of your house or apartment, because if they aren't, they may go knocking on your neighbours' doors instead of yours. This will happen from time to time however much you try to avoid it, but you don't want to become a nuisance to your neighbours. If you happen to have difficult neighbours who don't like you or who don't approve of what you are doing, you may have to consider finding somewhere else to work from. The actual type of property that you happen to be working from matters nought. We have known Readers who work in studio flats, large houses and everything in between.

The outside appearance of your place is reasonably immaterial, although common sense suggests that nobody will want to visit a dump, but some quite amazing disadvantages can be overcome if you have a good reputation. An example of this is our friend, Barbara Ellen, who ran an extremely successful consultancy in a top floor flat that could only be reached after climbing several outdoor flights of rickety iron stairs. Barbara is such a good Reader that even the extremely aged and those who hadn't used a muscle for years all managed the climb!

A place to work in

Any spare room can be turned into a wonderful consulting room. If you have no room to spare but you have a back yard or garden that is large enough to hold a construction of some kind, this may be a possibility. You might be able to put up a double-skinned shed, an enclosed gazebo (in warmer countries), or even find an old caravan and make that into a nice workroom, or you may be able to convert a garage for this purpose. If none of this is possible, there will probably be a room in your home that you don't use on a regular basis that can double up as a consulting room. Many Readers use a spare bedroom, with the bed covered by attractive "throws" and cushions when it is not in use.

If you can't designate a special room for your work, then make use of what you have. There are plenty of successful Consultants who have only one living room and they manage very well with this. One particularly successful lady that we used to know sat her clients at her kitchen table. Sasha remember times when her work-room was out of action due to being decorated, and she gave readings in the kitchen or the living room. On one unforgettable occasion when the hallway was being decorated, a client called Sheila Dunning and Sasha - plus tape-recorder and Tarot cards - all piled onto the middle of the bed! Clients understand what is like to have the house turned upside down on occasion and they are always surprisingly accommodating about this. Their main purpose after all, is not to assess your house for its beauty and elegance, but to have their reading. This doesn't mean that you should permanently live or work in a mess, and we will soon see there is plenty you can do to create the right kind of atmosphere.

> *Sasha's stories...*
>
> For many years I used what was supposed to be a dining room. We ate in the kitchen but at Christmas or on the occasions that we gave dinner parties we were able to turn the room back into a temporary dining room again. Jan and I now have two rooms in our flat that are specifically used as offices. When I give my occasional reading, I do so in my office and when we have guests to stay, we throw a roll-up futon on my office floor.

If you can afford to keep a room solely for the purpose of work then great, but if you can't, you will have to compromise a little. At the end of the day, the way you decorate your room and the furniture that you choose for it is entirely up to you. If you can't make special provisions for your work, then at least keep your surroundings clean and comfortable. There are absolutely no rules to follow except for the fact that if you feel comfortable, so will your clients. If you want lavender walls, Feng-Shui objects, lots of lighted candles, Mexican rugs and prints of angels and dolphins on the walls, go for it! If you don't, then don't.

Our friend Robert Currey, who runs the Equinox organisation and the Astrology Shop in Covent Garden in London, is well known for being a very stylish person. Robert's Libran Sun is expressed in just about everything that he does. The same applies to his Gemini wife Diane. His shop, his goods and even his paperwork tell of the thought that he puts into it all, and of the trouble he and Diane go to, in order to make everything look good - and it pays off. Robert suggests that your workroom must have a peaceful atmosphere and it must look and smell good. Robert suggests that you keep fresh flowers in your room and that you never smoke in it. My friend Jonathan Dee (who has Venus in Libra) hates cut flowers as they die! (Jan sympathises with this view... typical men who can't be bothered to water and change the flowers...). Jon suggests pot plants with plenty of greenery, some lovely pictures on the walls and plenty of ashtrays, as he a smoker and most of his clients seem also to smoke! So, you pays your money and you takes your choice!

> ### Sasha's stories...
>
> My workroom is basically an office, but yes, I have cut flowers and pot planets in it, for my own pleasure as well as for those who visit me. I also have interesting pictures on the walls, amusing objects, crystals, Tarot cards, computer disks and even a toy bat which we just know takes off every Halloween and comes back groggy and worn out on All Souls morning!

Your own appearance

Another thought from Robert Currey is that your own appearance needs a little consideration. You need to be clean, tidy and well dressed. Robert suggests that you need to be at least as well dressed as your clients. A formal suit and tie are not essential for a male Reader, and a female need not dress like a bank manager, but neither does either sex need to dress up in some kind of peculiar gypsy or "spiritual" outfit. Nice clothes of an ordinary kind are fine. There is nothing wrong with wearing jeans as long as they are clean and tidy. Many British female consultants seem to wear smart skirts and slacks teamed with smart shirts or interesting sweaters, while some wear floaty, slightly "hippie" outfits, complete with crystal or other necklaces, and that is also nice.

Most male readers wear jeans or slacks with coloured shirts and waistcoats or sweaters, and they rarely wear ties. Some men wear a necklace with an emblem or a crystal on it and that is also good. In short, do your own thing, but ensure that you are clean and tidy and that your hair looks good. Psychics probably shower and bathe more often than civilians anyway; it is the best way to keep our auras clear of psychic mess, so we usually look clean and smell clean and perfumed.

A few essentials

If you are a pure clairvoyant or a psychometrist, you won't need any special furniture, but if you read cards, runes, sand and so forth, you will need a table. If your table is a bit boring, a trip to your local craft market will offer you a terrific choice of table coverings. If you like candles, incense and so on, use them. As you will see in another chapter, a candle can even be used as a timing device! If you want to play "meditation music" on your CD, do so. If you don't wish to do any of these New Age things, then don't. The really important thing is the standard of your readings.

Palmists need a very good light to work in, while astrologers or any others who have to look at charts or even cards must be able to see what they are doing. Ensure that you have the right kind of lighting for your job, or you will strain your eyes and you may even miss vital information about your client. Nowadays clients expect you to give them a tape-recording of their reading, and they find this very helpful to them in the months that follow their visit to you. You will need a decent machine and a microphone arrangement that is comfortable for you. You don't have to buy the most expensive machine or the most expensive tapes on the market, but if you buy the cheapest of the cheap, you and your clients will be disappointed with the results.

Sasha's stories...

Of all the thousands of tapes that I have handed out, only one ever caused me a problem. This arose when a woman who was fighting with her husband took the tape of her reading home and edited it so that it sounded really nasty, and then she played it to him. The husband later came along to pick a fight with me about what he had heard on the tape. I handled the problem, and wondered what went on when he got back home...

Food and drink

You are not running a cafe, restaurant or any other kind of facility, so you don't actually need to do anything for your clients other than to give them a reading. However, if the appointment is likely to take some time, you may wish to make your client comfortable by offering them a drink and maybe a biscuit, especially if you fancy something yourself. If the day is hot, always offer your client a cold drink; he or she will be grateful.

Smoking

If you are a smoker, it is probably best these days to wait until you have a break and then to go into the kitchen and have a cigarette while making a cuppa. If you don't see many clients in one day and you happen to have one with you who is also a smoker, by all means share a sociable smoke when you take a breather. Bear in mind the damage that a client's cigarette can do, because believe it or not, a negligent client can easily burn your expensive dining table! Better perhaps to keep your own and your clients' cigarettes out of the workroom after all. To be honest, when you think about it, all of this is really down to common sense.

Drinking

Never drink alcohol just before or when you work. Don't drink, whether you are at home, at a festival or in any other location. If your clients smell drink on you, you soon won't have any clients left. If you are seen drinking at a festival, the organisers may ban you from future ones. A lunchtime beer may be acceptable, but our

Sasha's stories...
Your loo
   One Reader whom I consulted during my early days in this profession, used her downstairs hallway as a waiting room. At the time I was highly amused to see a number of well-made plastic signs artfully placed on her stairs showing her prices and details about her readings. The best sign of all proclaimed in large letters that use of her loo was strictly forbidden! Fortunately, this Reader lived just off a busy high street with a public loo close by.

advice is to leave all drinking until you have finished your work for the day, and then open a bottle of your favourite brew and go for it!

   The use of your own lavatory is an important matter to consider and believe it or not, this is quite a tricky one. Many clients will have come quite a long way to see you and they may need the loo, while others are nervous when they arrive and this will also affect their bladders. It would be churlish not to allow them to take a leak, but be careful how you arrange this. If you have a downstairs loo that is close to your office this is fine, but if your clients have to run upstairs or wander unsupervised through your house, you may have a problem. In such a case, make sure that the doors in your house are closed and, if possible, also locked. Clients can be light-fingered or they can be friends and relatives of thieves, and you don't want to allow them pinch anything or to assess your premises or your possessions for a future break-in. You just don't know, and especially if you are on your own, you shouldn't take unnecessary chances.

   Obviously you must keep your loo clean and make sure that there is sufficient paper in it, but you don't need to provide a bin for sanitary stuff. People being what they are, you can expect "accidents" of one kind or another, especially if they bring children with them, so don't be surprised if you have to disinfect the place on occasion. One sad client who was on some kind of heavy tranquilliser and who unfortunately also had her menstrual period at the time of her visit, left her Reader with the chore of clearing up the mess after she left. These days bleach, rubber gloves and disinfectant may actually save your life!

If you are totally neurotic about disease you had better reconsider your decision to be in this business in the first place, because just like any doctor, hairdresser, shop assistant or traveller on packed tube trains, you will be exposed to colds, flu and maybe even a few worse ailments. When AIDS first came into being, Sasha consulted a specialist doctor and asked him about the dangers, and he said that apart from using rubber gloves to clean the loo with and keeping it bleached clean and spotless, there weren't any. Obviously one should keep up to date with current developments, so by all means check with your own doctor for specific information as to keeping hygienic standards and arrangements. If using your own cups for your clients bothers you, get cups for their use and keep them separate.

Clients with children

If your client brings a child along, common sense will also dictate how you deal with this. Small children often sit with their mothers, while older ones can be sent off to your waiting area and given a magazine to read. If you know and trust your client, then let an older youngster sit in another room and watch your television.

If Jan or I were to give more than the occasional reading nowadays, we would ask our clients to wait in the hallway and we would provide a couple of folding chairs for the purpose. You must bear in mind that you cannot keep an eye on these waiting folk, so your household doors must be firmly shut or even locked, and if you have anything at all valuable it must be kept out of sight. Locks on your bedroom or living room doors may seem extreme, but they can save you a great deal of grief in the long run. We are not paranoid about theft, it is simply that we have experienced this on more than one occasion. Similarly, one doesn't take out life assurance because one expects a mishap, it is just sensible to do so. Books are a good target, especially if someone is interested in esoteric subjects, because pinching one or two of yours saves them from having to search for the books for themselves or of course, to pay for them! A fellow Reader recently told us that she has lost quite a few books to light-fingered clients, and I (Sasha) have lost ornaments and even a camera in this way! We really do advise you to have the contents of your house well insured, as you can then easily replace broken or stolen objects if the need arises.

Sasha's stories...
Your waiting area

I have known Readers who won't allow a client who arrives too early into their premises. Having a specific room to work in is luxury enough for most Readers, but having a waiting room as well is often out of the question. In one of my previous homes, I had a conservatory with some nice garden chairs in it, and that was a terrific place in which to keep my clients waiting. At other times, I have allowed certain clients to sit in my living room, and my family often had company with them while they were watching the TV of an evening. My children later told me that some of these folk irritated them, but otherwise there were no problems.

Insurance and other protection

Whatever your way of life, it makes sense to insure the contents of your home, but if you have clients coming in and out of the place, this is essential. The chances of having things taken from your home by clients is pretty low, (especially of you take the precautions that we have suggested), but if you are insured then there is a reasonable chance that you will be able to recover the cost of anything that does "walk". It is unlikely that a client will tell a potential burglar about your home and its contents but it can happen, and in such a case you need to be able to replace your missing goods. Make sure you let the insurer know you work from home; this will very likely mean a slightly higher premium, but then you won't have any claims disallowed.

The loneliness of the long distance Reader

One strange point is that if you spend too much time at home you can become lonely, isolated and even agoraphobic! You may have clients dancing in and out of your place hour after hour, but they are not company! Clients come to see you because they need a reading. Many of them will decide that you are their friend - mainly because you are the only person who appears to take a real interest in them and in their problems. But they are not *your* friends! Fair enough, some clients may eventually become personal friends, but the number who do so is likely to be very few indeed. This means that despite the fact that you may meet many people during the course of your working day, you can become very lonely!

For this reason, it is worth considering doing some of your readings outside the home and in the company of other Readers. A weekend at a psychic fair - especially if this is away from home - gives you a chance to mix with others in the same line as yourself, and to spend time "talking shop" and trading useful information. This kind of networking is often a very important part of any kind of job, so if you can do it yourself from time to time, it will recharge your psychic batteries. Try to have a social life or hobbies that take you out of your home if you can, as this too will lessen the feelings of isolation.

When we mentioned agoraphobia we were not kidding; it is peculiar how this insidious malaise can creep up on you, but if you don't get out into the real world frequently enough, you can eventually become afraid to do so! Try to leave your house for a while every day if you can, even if only to pop out to the shops for a pint of milk and a packet of ciggies, because this could save your sanity. This is a problem for writers as well as for consultants, so if you don't mind waiting a while, we will leave you for an hour now while we take ourselves off to the post office!

One final idea is to put up a few mirrors here and there, as seeing yourself reflected in them will make you feel less isolated. However, where mirrors are concerned, you must take the effects of Feng Shui into consideration, as a badly placed mirror can do more harm than good.

So let us look at yet another checklist and also consider a few final details before leaving this chapter.

Have you a suitable space to work in?	__Y/N__
Do you have a workable phone and communications arrangement?	__Y/N__
Is your house reasonably thief-proof?	__Y/N__
Do you have convenient "conveniences", or will your clients have to disappear upstairs to visit your loo?	__Y/N__
If you are woman who is alone in the house, do you want to see male clients?	__Y/N__
If you are a man, are you likely to be unfairly blamed for sexual harassment?	__Y/N__
Can you accommodate clients who want to bring children with them?	__Y/N__
Does your family feel comfortable about you giving readings from home?	__Y/N__
Can you fit your hours around the needs of your family?	__Y/N__
Does your family support/help you in doing this work from home?	__Y/N__
Will you feel lonely or isolated if you spend too much time at home?	__Y/N__
Totals:	__Y/N__

Your answers to these questions will give you food for thought in many cases, but remember that with a bit of perseverance, there is always a way around a few obstacles. Too many, however, and perhaps you'll need to reconsider the idea of working from home.

Chapter 6

LOCATION, FAMILY LIFE, RELATIONSHIPS AND SEXUAL PERIL

Family life – some alternatives – family friction – hours of work – spiritual incompatibility – a classic true story – dangerous situations – sensible solutions

We have tucked this chapter in after the previous one that focuses upon working from home, as it relates to the home environment, but in an emotional manner rather than in a practical one.

Sasha's stories...

Family life

My first husband, Tony, never minded having people trooping through our home for consultations whether he was there or not. He was happy for me to use my work room for readings and teaching, and he was perfectly at ease at the sight of a dozen folk wandering up and down our garden with dowsing rods in their hands. Tony chatted amiably to clients and students alike and nothing fazed him.

My second husband, Jan, is a little more territorial about his home but he has become accustomed to having the odd client and my astrology classes in the flat, and he no longer feels uncomfortable with the situation. Until we got together, Jan lived exclusively in Africa and in those countries, one needs to be far more careful about security than in the UK. Even so, we don't allow people to float around the place unsupervised, and I even take clients into the kitchen with me for a chat when I go to make them a cup of coffee. When I told my pal Robert Currey about this, he dryly commented that he hoped my kitchen was tidy. It is: with three planets in Virgo and one in Libra, I am not capable of living or working in a mess!

Consider some alternatives

If your work really does upset your family, then you will have to consider only working at such times when they are all out of the house or finding somewhere else to work from; however, if compromises can be made, being at home really is the least expensive and awkward option.

If you have to fight with the family to use the phone, you can put in a separate line for your business or you can use a mobile/cellphone. If the noise of the phone ringing when you are relaxing becomes a problem, you can buy the kind of phone that turns the ringer off and simply directs calls to an answering machine or even to an answering service. If you use a mobile phone, you can take it with you when you are out. It is now possible to have a phone that rings in a different way for different kinds of calls, so that you know which ones are work enquiries and which are for the family. More telephone innovations are coming on to the market every day now, and doubtless there will soon be even more advances in this area. It is actually possible now for your clients to make enquiries to book appointments by e-mail! We call this "she-mail" in our house, because Sasha uses it a great deal to keep in touch with her female friends who are overseas. We even do a little astrology on the she-mail these days!

Family friction

Some people don't mind their partners trotting off to psychic festivals and other events, and they are even sanguine about their partner staying away from home for a couple of nights here and there.

Others don't like it at all and they don't like going along to these events themselves either. Festivals are usually run over weekends, so if your spouse wants your company at that time, this may cause friction. If your partner is generally happy with the kind of work that you do but is unhappy with some of the arrangements that go along with it, you should be able to work out a compromise solution.

Hours of work

Sometimes you can rearrange the hours of your work to minimise interference with family life. This may mean that you are working while the family is digesting their dinner in front of the television but that may be a small sacrifice to make. You can always video a good programme and watch it at a time that is more convenient to you. You may work during the mornings when the house is quiet. If your children are young, you may choose to take a break from work during the school holidays. If your family wants your company during the weekends, then confine your work to weekdays, possibly working during one or two weekday evenings to accommodate those clients who can't get time off during the day. A bit of trial and error will soon show you what works best for you and for your family.

Spiritual incompatibility

Generally speaking, if a man is interested in astrology, Rune reading, healing or whatever, his partner will try to take an interest in it too. The aggravation usually occurs when it is the woman who leads a spiritual life, because some men really do balk against it. Some men perceive what we do as being weird, peculiar, embarrassing and even frightening. They aren't interested in the subject themselves and they don't want to hear about it. They hate seeing you do something that they can't do themselves, and they don't like the fact that others find you interesting. A partner may be desperately jealous of your abilities and of the attention and affection that this draws to you.

If you think that your interests are the only thorn in the side of your marriage, it will be up to you to work out ways of keeping the subject away from the end of your partner's nose. After all, if your partner is mad keen on football, tennis, singing, mending old cars or whatever, imagine how this would irritate you if it were going on under your nose all the time. Your relationship may be more important to you than your work - or not - as the case may be. Don't take what you do too seriously, but don't allow yourself to be bullied out of working. In some cases, all that is needed is a little consideration. Be prepared to give reasonable time to your job, your family, your friends and yourself. A juggling act indeed, but it may be the only way. However, if one person insists on having his or her own way at the expense of the other in any sphere of life - let alone a partner's job - this is obviously something that needs to be addressed. A sense of humour can often save the day and your spouse's references to you riding on a broomstick and waving your magic wand can and should be part of the fun. Constant nasty remarks are another matter, though.

Molly Ann Fairley's story

Molly Ann was married for many years to an uptight, pin-striped Capricorn business executive whose values and priorities were as distant from our spiritual world as it is possible to be. Molly Ann, being a Pisces with both Sagittarius and Aquarius strongly marked on her chart, may have started out life as a "normal person" but as the years rolled by, she (like so many of us) developed a strong interest in spiritual work. Molly Ann has been a teacher of yoga, a healer and a Reader for many years. True to the story of her birthchart, she has delved into just about every aspect of this work. Some of Molly Ann's past interests were so way out that even those who are reading this book might have wondered if she had been born on another planet! Imagine how her hubby, a man who needed a reliable hostess for his business colleagues, a good dinner on the table after his day in the office, a drink placed in his hand and a quality newspaper carefully folded and in position on the arm of his chair, must have felt like coping with our Molly Ann? She described to us in hilarious detail, the reaction one evening when her husband came home to find her suspended upside down on a revolving frame. She was dressed in a swimming costume and swimming cap, her body and hair thickly coated in therapeutic creams, while she meditated and developed her considerable spiritual powers. But let Molly Ann tell you the following story for herself.

I was giving lessons on a variety of physical and spiritual themes at home, and on this occasion our living room was filled with people lying on the floor in a minor state of semi-hypnotic trance while they were concentrating on their breathing. My husband arrived home a touch early from his office. He pulled me into the kitchen and asked, "What the hell are these people doing here?"

"Breathing." I replied.

"Well, if that is all they are doing, can't they go and breathe in the garden while you make my dinner?"

"They will all go home soon," responded Molly Ann, "and then I will make your dinner."

A few moments later, Molly Ann's class got up from the floor, and each one of them then gave her five pounds before leaving the house. Five pounds was a considerable amount of money in those days, and upon seeing a quantity of these notes pass into Molly Ann's hand, Mr. Capricorn decided that lessons on breathing were not such a bad thing after all - as long as his dinner could be organised and put in the oven beforehand!

To be honest, Jan the banker and Sasha the ex-secretary can see Mr. Capricorn's point of view, but we can also see Molly Ann's. These two were miles apart and the difficulty in either of them compromising made their marriage impossible. In Molly Ann's own words when she looks back to those early days, "the more rigid and conventional that he became, the more obstinately way-out I became, and vice versa."

Thus, Jan and Sasha feel that if compromise is truly impossible in a host of different areas of one's marriage (not only in a desire to do psychic work) the viability of such a relationship needs to be examined. We don't advocate divorce as the cure for every marital ill, but the yawning gulf between the spiritual and the non-spiritual person can lead to just that. Jan and I have both been married before and both of our previous partners are spiritual, so that was not the cause of our own problems.

A classic true story from Sasha

One case that I will never forget is that of a man called Giles. This chap came across my first Tarot book and he soon learned to read the cards. Giles discovered that he had psychic gifts and as a result, he dived pell-mell into the weirdest aspects of spiritualism, which he proceeded to take to insane lengths. To be honest, Giles had some kind of kink, so the spiritual stuff was only an outlet for something else that was intense and strange in his personality. Giles' wife was interested in horses, and she and their children spent most of their time at the local stables. The marriage gradually broke down and in the end it was a case of, "It's the spirits or me" on his wife's side and "It's the horses or me," on Giles' side. Needless to say, they divorced and went their own separate ways. Thus, if the differences between you and your partner are part of a wider problem within your relationship, going pell-mell into the spiritual life can kill it off completely! Many marriages have come to grief over this. The same can apply, of course, to other demanding jobs such as nursing. It isn't the job that's the problem, it's usually a latent incompatibility that surfaces in times of stress.

One real danger is to try to drag a partner into your world when he or she really doesn't want it. Naturally, you will want to answer any mild enquiry that your spouse or that any other member of your family brings up, but leave it at that. Another major danger occurs when someone starts a new relationship and then tries to push the new lover into becoming a fully-fledged reader, healer, astrologer, vegan, Spiritualist, meditator or anything else of the kind. Allow those who want to learn to do so, but don't push anything down anyone else's throat. Jan is an astrologer but he has never bothered to learn the Tarot or to read palms, and although he is intuitive and psychic to a high degree, his talents are different from Sasha's - and that is just fine by her. We are very fortunate in that our abilities complement each other's to a remarkable extent, which is not always that common. Also remember that however excited you are about your work or your interests, there is more to life, so try to lead a fully rounded family life. Do lots of other things and leave the subject of your work alone for much of the time.

Sasha's stories...
Now for the good news
Many happy relationships have been formed by people who have met through our kind of work. It was Jan's interest in astrology that brought him to a workshop that I was giving during my tour of South Africa, and that is how we met. However, we have plenty of other interests apart from our esoteric work to keep us busy.

Dangerous situations for female Consultants

Before leaving the subject of working from home, there is one more thing that we need to advise you about. If you are female, unattached or living alone, you may not wish to deal with male clients other than those who you know well and with whom you feel safe and happy to be alone. We doubt that the sight of a stream of strange men walking in and out of your house will give you a "red light" reputation, but it could put you in personal danger. The chances are that a male client has nothing further on his mind than having a good reading but you can't be sure, so think before you allow any old Tom, Dick or Harry into your abode. If you have a partner and/ or a family of older children, you can arrange to see your male clients when your loved ones are around the house. If you work partly from some other premises such as a space in a shop, then direct your male clients there, otherwise seriously consider whether you want to deal with men at all.

Dangerous situations for male Consultants

It is unlikely that a female client is going to accuse you of making sexual advances, but it may be worth finding ways of working where there are other people around. If you are married and your wife is pottering around the home this is fine, but if you are totally alone, you may consider working in some kind of centre where there are always others around.

Never say or do anything flirtatious or anything that could be construed as intimate, sexual or "coming-on" to a female client. Even a mild joke could be taken the wrong way, and anything further than this will get you into all kinds of deep waters. If your client starts to talk about her sex-life in any depth, gently cut her off and perhaps consider referring her to a female Reader or a counsellor. If you really fancy a client, then keep this to yourself. There are plenty of nice women around who aren't your clients, so if you are

---

Sasha's stories...

During my years of dealing with clients, I have been disconcerted a few times by males. Men can become extremely agitated if they are going through a difficult time in their lives, and if a reading brings unpleasant feelings to the fore, they can become quite frightening. I have to say that the only man who ever talked to me about sex in a slightly disconcerting way was an old boy who came to me on a fairly regular basis. One day, he admitted that he had always wanted to be a woman and that he liked to dress up in woman's clothes. This didn't worry me because he really was a soft old duck, but it could have been something much nastier.

---

looking for any kind of relationship, do this outside the realm of your work.

Sensible solutions

To sum up, the sensible solution is to try as far as possible to fit your work around your family responsibilities and to make life better rather than worse for all concerned. Keep yourself safe and don't ever lay yourself open to accusations of sexual harassment.

Chapter 7

WHEN YOU CAN'T WORK FROM YOUR HOME

Someone else's home – a local shop – a shopping mall – psychic fairs & festivals – telephone readings – postal readings – party plan readings – other exotic venues – readings at your other place of work – Barbara's story

Not everybody's home circumstances are conducive to running a consultancy, so in this chapter we will look into a number of alternatives. Even those of you who can work from home may fancy a change of scene from time to time, and you may wish to take advantage of some of the alternatives.

The following list runs through the kind of ideas that we will go into in this chapter.

- A friend's home.
- A local shop
- A shopping mall
- Psychic fairs
- Telephone readings (these can be done from any location)
- Postal readings
- Party-plan readings
- Other exotic venues: hotels, pubs, clubs, restaurants, formal office parties
- Readings at your other job: your office canteen during lunch hour
- Psychic centres, holistic centres, dial-a-psychic centres

A friend's home

If your home is no good as a workplace, you may have a friend who has a vacant room and who is happy to allow you to work from his or her premises. You can arrange to do this in return for an agreed fee or for a percentage of what you take from your readings. If you can't take bookings yourself, your friend may be able to do this for you, which means that you will have some clients lined up in advance.

If you haven't read through the chapter on working from home, do so now, because most of the points that we have covered will apply. For example, the accessibility of the location and the safety factor if you expect to be alone in the premises while working.

A local shop

You might contact a local shop that sells goods that are complementary to your work to see whether they would rent you a corner to work from. There are two ways of dealing with the payment for this, and the best one for you depends upon a variety of circumstances and the system that you and your hosts wish to use.

You can pay for your space on a straightforward rental basis, which means that both you and the shop know exactly what this will amount to, or you can pay the shop a percentage of the takings from each of your readings. The shopkeeper could display a permanent notice in the window of his shop, as this will bring in enquiries whether you are present or not. If the shop takes bookings for you, this means that you will have at least some of your hours accounted for before you arrive for your day's work. The shopkeeper is more likely to take an interest in booking people in for you if he is on a percentage of your takings. Bear in mind that if the shop gets very busy, the last thing the shop staff will want to be bothered with is making bookings for you. You may be happy for the shop staff to take bookings for you but Jan and I strongly advise you not to allow them to handle the actual money. Your colleagues may be dead honest and they may be wonderful bookkeepers and record keepers, but we have had experience of muddled bookkeeping (and worse), and you don't need to give away any of your precious income in this way. It is hard enough to earn a living without suffering losses, and being ripped off either by accident or on purpose leaves a really nasty taste.

If you equip yourself with a mobile/cell phone, you can take your own bookings, whether you are actually at the shop or not. This will give you flexibility so that you can organise your life any way that you want, and this puts you in total control of your clients and your income. Telephone technology is improving all the time and today's voice mail means that you can handle almost anything at any time and any place. As the public gets to know your routine, a few clients will turn up on spec hoping to be able to see you. Hopefully, there will also be a few "impulse buyers" as well.

> **Tip:**
> If you want to be able to take bookings by phone at any time, make sure this point is clearly shown on your notices and other advertising material.

> **Tip:**
> Perhaps the shop personnel can hand out business cards and leaflets for you.
> If you decide to rent a corner of a shop, you will need a very good notice outside to attract the attention of passers by. A board that stands up on legs outside the shop is a good idea, but this may be inconvenient or even illegal if the shop is in a narrow or busy high street location. A shopping arcade or a mall of some kind might be the best location.

It is not worth approaching a busy shop, as they won't need or want you there. A fairly quiet venue won't bring you much passing trade, but it could be useful if you advertise your services in a variety of places and not just in the window of the shop itself. A very quiet place that people don't normally visit at all probably isn't much use. A friend of ours once rented space at a very dead antiques market and found this to be a total waste of time, money and energy.

Wherever you work, try to do so out in the open where you can be seen plying your trade. It is perfectly natural for all concerned to think that your clients prefer privacy and a nice quiet screened off area at the back of the shop or upstairs in the store room, but this does nothing for your marketing. You must sit in an open position right up front so that passers-by can see you working. Potential clients will either make a mental note of your presence or ring for an appointment at some other time. If you can combine your shop work with time spent working from a more secluded venue, you can hand out cards and literature. This means that clients who feel that they need more privacy than the local shopping mall can arrange to come and see you at a later date.

A shopping mall

This can sometimes be an excellent opportunity, as the mall owners often like anything that either draws people to the mall or that keeps them around longer. There may be other small stalls of one sort or another at a mall convenient to you and it is well worth while trying to get a spot for yourself. With lots of pedestrian traffic passing by, there is opportunity for business, there is reasonable safety through being in a public area, and you can also easily buy your daily shopping at the same time!

Walk around and see if you can find a spot that is not too draughty, that is reasonably quiet (so that your clients can hear you...), and that isn't in a bottleneck where people will bump into your stand. Check whether you will be allowed to put up some sort of stand, preferably with partitioning that will give a bit of privacy. We have a mall near to us in Ealing Broadway, where there are a number of small "booths" actually built into one of the passageways, that are ideal for this kind purpose. No doubt there's a waiting list for these spots, but that's to be expected.

Psychic fairs and festivals

Psychic fairs and festivals are worth considering, sometimes not so much for the money that you make there and then, as for the opportunity these give you to hand out business cards and leaflets about yourself and your services. Psychic fairs vary greatly in their size, scope and effectiveness, but the really large ones may be out of your league due to the cost of renting a stand. The prestigious annual Mind, Body and Spirit Festival in London has one large stand of Readers, but this is rented by the British Astrological and Psychic Society who only allow those Consultants who have been vetted by their organisation to work there. There are a few other readers scattered around the place but they are also on stands that are attached to specific organisations. Much the same goes for the festivals in Sydney and Melbourne, because their Readers' stand also belongs to a specific society.

Smaller fairs will be happy to let you rent a table but they may want some assurance that you know your job. Space rental varies tremendously, as do the number of people who the organisers get through the door. You can find out what Readers charge at such events by visiting one yourself and taking a look around. In our experience, there is a kind of optimum fee that all the Readers at the fair charge, but as this can change from fair to fair, you should take a fibre-tipped pen, some card and perhaps a plastic stencil set along so that you can make a notice up on the spot. Such fairs are excellent training grounds even for an experienced Reader, because you will deal with whoever shows up for a reading and you will also have to cope with noise and other distractions.

If you try your hand at fairs, make sure that you have plenty of business cards and other literature to hand out, as this is the greatest benefit that you will derive from this exercise. The cost of getting to the venue, renting space and carting your equipment to the site will eat up a fair bit of time, money and energy, but as long as the fair is reasonably local to your place of work, the exposure will make it worthwhile. Think carefully before agreeing to take space at a fair that is at a distance, as the cost of travel and accommodation will reduce your financial returns. However, if the fair is well run and well attended, it still may be worth doing.

Those of you who are astrologers have an advantage at such fairs, now that there are some excellent report programs available for your computer. Using one of these programs, you can deal with a far greater number of clients, as you only need to key in the birth details and then wait for the few minutes that it takes your printer to print out the report. Equinox do this regularly at the larger festivals, and although you can't buy their program, there are others available. The two with which Jan and I have had some experience are the Solar Fire®, and Matrix®, report writers. These are both of a professional standard and are readily available in the UK and the USA, as well as many other countries. Various others are available at various price ranges, but as always, you get what you pay for, and it is worth getting the best you can afford. You can use such programs for postal readings as well, but remember that your charges should be lower for such readings than for a normal consultation - there is still no computer that can match the human brain in delivering a full consultation, whether astrological, Tarot (yes, there are Tarot programs available as well), or any other kind. This naturally is reflected in what the public will pay, or should be expected to pay. As we've mentioned previously, always look into what your income is likely to be from this source before lashing out all your spare cash on an expensive computer program.

If you have anything to sell at such a fair, then this adds interest to your stand, but this really becomes a two-handed venture because you will need someone to sell the goods while you do the readings. It is impossible to concentrate on readings and sell goods at the same time. You cannot give your attention to two clients at the same time, don't even think about it! Just put yourself into the client's position, and imagine how you would feel if your reading were to be interrupted every few minutes. If you are selling anything of value, you absolutely must have someone else on the stand to look after your stock, to prevent it from "walking" off the stand.

If you enjoy teaching or demonstrating your skills, you can offer to give a talk. This is always useful as a few members of your audience are likely to come along to your stand for a reading after your talk. Never be pushed into giving the last talk of the day because there will be no time to cash in on this or to speak to anyone afterwards. Once again, if you give a talk, ensure that a leaflet giving your details reaches each person who comes in. Bear in mind that if you have to leave your stand in order to give a lecture or for any other reason, you must have someone on hand to guard your possessions.

You can often rent a space that is large enough for two or three people to share at such fairs. This not only helps you to deal with the above-mentioned problems but it can be much more cost effective than renting an individual stand. Going along with a friend means that you share the expense and the effort of getting yourself and your stuff to and from the venue, and it also means that you have someone to chat to during slack moments. We will come back to the topic of psychic fairs and festivals a little later in this book, as this method of working has many advantages, but it does bring its own special problems and there are a whole gamut of things for you to take into account.

Telephone readings

One clever method of working is to give telephone readings and while many Readers turn away this kind of work, there are definite benefits if you do it right. You don't need a special place to work from and you don't even need to get dressed if you don't want to! Tarot readings, rune readings, astrology, numerology, graphology and many other forms of divination can be done over the phone. It is easy to lose money on this kind of reading but there are two simple steps that you can take to prevent this from happening.

If a client contacts you for a phone reading, she may well expect you to give your reading, there and then, but you must make it clear that this is not how the system works. You must ask the client to send you the money for the reading in advance. If your clients send cheques, you must allow enough time for each cheque to arrive at your address and then to be cleared through the banking system and reach your account. A UK bank takes five to seven working days to clear a cheque (working days are Monday to Friday). This means that at least a week will need to elapse from the time of the booking to the actual reading. You may want to check with your bank that the client's cheque has cleared your account. If you do a lot of this kind of work, you can arrange to have weekly bank statements, but this will increase your bank charges, so you should take this into account when pricing your readings. If the client sends you a postal order or some kind of money order that can be cashed immediately, then obviously you can do the reading as soon as you receive it. If you decide to trust a caller to have a reading first and then to send the money on to you, experience shows that there is about a ten per cent chance that he or she will actually do so! To amend an old saying slightly, a good motto would be: "In God we trust, everyone else pays cash up front". If you still feel unhappy about being so "hard", look at it this way: that is the way everyone else does business, and they wouldn't be doing it if it wasn't necessary. Having worked your overheads (rent, equipment costs, stationery, advertising costs and income tax, etc.) into the price of a reading, let's say that, for example, you are making in round figures £5 ($8) actual profit per £20 ($30) reading. With one unpaid debt, you have to do four more readings just to get back to square one! (This is Jan writing here, by the way, and this is exactly the kind of advice I used to give my banking clients, whatever line of business they were in...). Bad debts are expensive, even if you can set some of them off against tax.

You must be happy with this kind of work or you will spend more unnecessary time and money sending money back to your clients after readings that fail. Even a good Reader has the occasional "blowout", so you need to face the fact that there will be the occasional refund to be processed.

Your client needs to know that it is he or she who will make the phone call, as this simply can't land up on your phone bill. Clients can phone you from long distances and unbelievably, they can stay on the phone to you for an amazing length of time. It is a fact that when a needy client finds a sympathetic Consultant on the end of her phone, she won't care how long the reading takes. Despite the fact that this kind of work is cost effective, your time is still valuable (and so is the client's phone bill), so you may wish to call a halt after whatever period of time that you have allowed for the reading has passed.

Most Consultants charge far less for phone readings than they do for the clients they see in person. The logic behind this is that a phone reading is destined to be a "quicky" as opposed to a full-blown personal appointment, but in our experience, clients will sit on the phone for as long as they feel inclined to. Therefore the time you spend on this can be much the same as you would spend with a client who visits you in person, and the skills that you use are exactly the same, so why charge less?

Some Readers really do need to have their client in the room with them so that they can create a psychic link. Others only feel comfortable when they can visually monitor the client's reaction to the reading. We can only suggest that you give phone readings a try, and if you find that you are not comfortable working this way, then forget it.

Tip

Phone work can suit graphologists and astrologers who work on a scientific vibration rather than a psychic one. It can also suit those psychics who are happy to hold a photograph of the client or of anybody that the client wishes to know more about. In these cases, charts will have to be made up in advance and handwriting or photos will need to be sent in beforehand.

Some divinations simply don't lend themselves to telephone work. Palmistry is an obvious one. It is possible to instruct a client to take a palm print with lipstick and then to send it to you through the post, but such prints are always pretty awful. Also, so much that is on the backs of the hands, the nails, the shape of the hand and so on are lost. Photocopies of hands are hopeless.

For those who enjoy telephone work, these days there are organisations that you can join which will advertise for clients and arrange for them to call you at pre-arranged times. Naturally, such organisations split the fee that the client pays and you only get a percentage, but this can be worth doing as a top-up to other forms of reading work.

Postal readings

Astrology, numerology, graphology, the Tarot, the Runes, dream interpretations and a variety of other divinations can be carried out by post. An astrology or numerology reading can be put on tape or typed out, but you will need to consider the amount of time that typing is likely to take you. Your client won't be able to ask specific questions or guide you to the particular matters that are on his mind, so you may feel that there is a limited appeal for postal readings. Worse still working in a vacuum of this kind is strangely frustrating and also boring. However, there are times when this method is worth considering as the following story demonstrates.

Sasha's stories...

Many years ago, I worked every Saturday in a psychic centre in a London hotel. The cost of renting my table, getting to the venue and paying for car parking ate up all that I earned during my Saturdays, but I picked up a great deal of astrology work that I could take home, prepare and produce and then bring back in the following week. I guess I used this Saturday job as a form of self-financed marketing, because the readings that I did on the spot paid my expenses and the stuff that I worked on at home made money.

We must mention a couple of pitfalls. Firstly, never send out anything to anybody without getting the money for it up-front. Secondly, if you copy what Sasha did at the psychic centre and take orders for material to be brought in the following week, you must either ensure that this is paid for up-front or that at least half the fee is left with you as a deposit. The impulse to have a reading may pass after a week, and the client may never bother to turn up to collect the work. This scenario is a soul-destroying one, and costly.

We seriously suggest that you avoid doing charts or written or packaged readings for any kind of third party. Someone may decide that a packaged reading would be just the right birthday present for their friend or as a terrific "thank you" to someone who has done them a favour. If you can supply a commercial computerised horoscope report package or something similar, this is borderline, because these products are all relatively vague and innocuous, but a "real" reading is a different matter. We sincerely feel that a reading should be requested by the person who has it, and that any reading should only be given to a person who really wants one. What do you say if you discover that the recipient of this "gift" has a truly crappy year ahead of him? Do you lie? Do you tell all? Do you phone the friend who requested the service and tell them, in the hope that they will have the sense not to pass on this juicy piece of information? The whole scenario gives us goose pimples. If someone insists on this service, you should insist right back that the designated recipient is told about it and that they contact you personally and authorise you to go ahead with the job. And you should send the tape or report direct to the recipient, not to the person paying for it - a reading is personal, and only the recipient can decide whether to share it, after he or she has digested the contents. In any event, a person who hasn't actually requested a reading won't value it.

Party plan readings

One rather pleasant way of working is when someone asks a few friends round and then employs you as the reader for the evening. There are various ways you can approach this. Firstly, you may give a little talk to the assembled company followed by a few readings, or you can simply make yourself comfortable in another room and see each client one after another. You will need to work out a reasonable time-scale for the job and a reasonable price for each reading, and you may decide to give the hostess a freebie as part of the package. These days most people expect to have their reading taped, so you will either have to take a tape recorder with you or ensure that your hostess has a good one that she can lend you for the occasion. Also ensure that you have sufficient tapes available for the number of clients you expect to see and perhaps one or two extra. Party-plan reading is hard work but it is enjoyable because the clients are in a mild form of party mode. When you have finished your evening's work, you will doubtless be able to have a drink, a snack and a chat to the party clients.

Your readings will need to be fairly short and sweet, so you will doubtless charge quite a bit less than you would if each client visited your home separately, but this usually turns out to be worth the effort from a financial point of view. Ensure that there will be a sensible number of clients on hand for readings, because too few makes the trip a waste of time. On the other hand, too many clients means that you will either be sitting in your party-planner's house until three in the morning, or some clients will have to go away disappointed.

There are only two drawbacks to this kind of work that we can think of. The first is that it is quite tiring to do a number of readings one after another, especially as this work invariably occurs during the evening. The second is that you may have difficulty in actually finding the location, especially as the night in question will definitely be dark, wet and dismal. It may be a good idea to have someone fetch you and return you after the event, but this means that you will have to wait for a lift back home afterwards. Having your own transport means that you can slope off as soon as you have finished working, and avoid socialising

Tip

There is nothing to stop you trying a combination of all these methods or choosing those that suit you best. If I were a full time reader now, I would see clients at home, work over the phone, do some readings by post, do party-plan readings and visit psychic fairs - if only to take myself out of the house from time to time.

with the party-goers if you don't feel like being sociable, or if you're short of time.

Sasha's stories...
Other exotic venues

Don't turn your nose up at the idea of giving readings at your local school's fete. Sitting in a tent for an afternoon doing quick readings and then giving the money you take to the school may not appear to be a great commercial success, but it offers you a magnificent opportunity to dish out business cards and leaflets. Business cards and literature will lead to follow-up readings as long as the school is close to your usual place of work.

Sometimes a local firm will hire you as a kind of entertainer at a function. I have done readings at radio stations, newspaper offices, employment agencies and all manner of dinner dances. Sometimes I have been the only Consultant present and sometimes there have been a few of us dotted around the place. On one Halloween evening, I was even given a witch's hat to wear for the occasion! My friend, the lovely John Lindsay, and I had a little job in a nightclub which we did once a month over a period of about two years. The nightclub's management paid us a set fee for each night's work, so we never had to worry about the number of clients who were likely to turn up. As it happens, we were always packed out with business from the moment we arrived until the club shut in the early hours of the following morning. The clients paid nothing for their readings as this was part of the "entertainment" that was put on by the club.

There are hotels and other public places such as restaurants that might be happy to put on an event. You may be the only Reader on hand or the affair could be something much more ambitious, such as three or four consultants, each offering a different kind of reading. Some hotels are very happy to put on a weekend event during their off-season as this brings in business for them. Such an event can include lectures, demonstrations and readings. If you have a flair for organisation and enough salesmanship and sheer chutzpah to get a hotel involved in such a scheme, it could work well and it could even become a regular event. I remember that in the case of the one that I attended, I was paid a set fee for my lectures and then a percentage of the fees that they charged for my readings. All the bookings, details and money were handled by a treasurer, but I kept a note of what I had done to ensure that it tallied with what I was paid after the event. It worked just fine.

Talk things over with other Consultants, because they may have some ideas that we haven't come across. There may be some novel notions that are specific to your location or your particular situation. For example, one particularly enterprising Aries lady from Southend called Lindsey, is a hairdresser who has now taken up astrology and the Tarot. Lindsey works at both of these occupations at her home on a part-time basis. This gives her working life a bit of variety, and as her clients for both jobs tend to be women, they cross over from one service to another. Lindsey says that her only problem is that she has to designate days for one kind of work or the other because otherwise she has to sweep all the reading stuff away when a hair client comes and vice versa. She says that after a perm, the place is filled with the pong of ammonia, which doesn't quite match the usual incense-filled atmosphere of psychic and astrological readings!

Readings at your other place of work

A surprising number of people start out as professionals by giving readings at their place of work during their lunch hour. This may be a fun thing to do once in a while and it will generate some useful interest, especially if you are just starting out as a Reader, but in our opinion this method of working has some drawbacks that we cover elsewhere in this book.

If it appears that it would be all right to give the odd reading from a corner table in your works canteen, it might actually be worth doing a few free or very inexpensive readings just to get your name round. When you have become more experienced and confident in your abilities and things look as if they are going to pick up, stop your activities, hand out business cards and suggest that those who want to consult you do so on a professional basis and at another venue.

Barbara's story

Our friend Barbara Ellen is a psychic who travels the world with her work. Barbara arranges for a local person to advertise the fact that she will be in town ahead of time and this agent also takes advance bookings for her. Barbara arrives, sits down and works through a load of clients one after another for several days, and then she stops work, socialises, sight sees and generally enjoys being wherever she is. Barbara has literally girdled the earth many times by this means, working in such diverse places as different parts of America, in Japan, Malta, Hong Kong, Hawaii and just about everywhere else in between. She even works here in the UK from time to time. If you enjoy travelling, then this is the way to do it. However, Barbara has the relevant visas, tax arrangements and green cards, etc. that enable her to do this work overseas, and if you wish to emulate Barbara, you must make such arrangements for yourself. These are specialised requirements that go well beyond the scope of this book, so you would have to contact the embassies or consulates of the countries involved for detailed guidance.

Chapter 8

COMBINING DIFFERENT JOBS

Health & Healing - teaching - keep it simple - venues for your work - adult institutions & regular schools - the world of commerce - job applications - lectures & demonstrations - dial a psychic phone lines - lecturing - broadcasting

The vast majority of Consultants have a "day job", or what Jan calls a "proper job", in addition to giving readings. Most people need a reliable income to pay their bills with, and then use their reading skills to top this up. Others fit in readings with part time work or with full time motherhood. It doesn't matter whether you are a plumber, a clerk, a banker or a brain surgeon, if you take any money for readings you are also a professional Reader. Whether you declare this to the tax man or not is your business, but there are dangers in working on the side in the "black economy" as you will see when we reach the chapter on tax and social security.

If your consultancy is your full time job, you can add complementary or ancillary jobs to this, and this chapter looks into a few possibilities in this arena.

The field of health and healing

Whilst gathering information for this book, Jan and I have discovered that a large number of Readers are also Healers or Therapists. Combining these two skills can be an ideal mix because in many cases the client who needs a reading also needs healing or therapy of some kind, and vice versa. Spiritual healing is a natural partner to the business of giving readings, because practically every

Reader can heal through some form of channelling if they put their minds to it. Not all Readers wish to charge for this service, preferring to offer their channelling abilities as a kind of gift from Spirit. Those who have become properly trained, qualified and registered as healers will charge for their services as this is an important part of their work.

Readers may be trained and qualified Therapists and Therapists may also be Readers. These two services can be offered as separate entities or as a package, depending upon what the client needs. The combination of working as a Therapist and as a Reader is an excellent one, as a Reader's client may only want to consult the Reader once a year whilst therapy can be an on-going matter. In short, it is probably easier to earn a living as a Therapist than as a Reader. If you are into therapy of any kind, this probably ought to be your first line of operation, with readings being on offer as a secondary service for those clients who specifically request it. Having said that, if you have a client who only needs a reading and who neither needs nor wants healing or therapy, don't force your other skills upon them. You may reach a stage where some clients only come to you for treatment while others only consult you for readings. Whatever works for you and your client is right.

Therapy can include anything from hypnotherapy, aromatherapy, massage, herbalism, Chinese medicine, reflexology, kinesiology or any number of other alternative practices, but while some therapies mix well with a reading consultancy, others don't. Osteopaths, chiropractors and homeopaths are almost part of the normal medical "establishment" these days and they couldn't include anything as "flaky" as a Tarot reading as any part of a consultation. Another difficult area is that of psychotherapy, as this is also considered to be a "respectable" area of operation. However, some clients are sufficiently switched on to esoteric work to welcome a reading as part and parcel of their treatment.

Teaching

Many Readers thoroughly enjoy teaching and passing on their skills and knowledge to others. If this applies to you, teaching is a pleasant way of earning money, meeting nice people and of working on a different "vibration" to that which is required for your readings. If you do any kind of clairvoyant or healing work, you may find that it eventually begins to drain you, especially if you have a run of "heavy" or difficult clients, so having something quite different to turn to can be a nice change of pace. You may not earn as much money from teaching as you do by giving readings, but as long as something useful is coming in from it, it is worthwhile. However, there are ways of losing money even by doing something this straightforward, so we will look at ways to maximise your potential and to minimise your losses.

Keep it simple

Years ago I remember a chap telling me that he had started a class for astrology students and that over 60 people had turned up for the first session. I remember being very impressed by this at the time, but this conversation took place in the 1970s when astrology was just beginning to take off and when there was very little in the way of education or books available. With the 20/20 hindsight of experience, I know that it is impossible to teach astrology to a class of that size and that people will soon drift away if they don't get the individual attention that they need. In short, I doubt that this man's students stayed with him for long enough to complete a course. Nowadays, six to sixteen people is a more realistic number to expect, and to be able to deal with successfully.

Venues for your work

The cheapest and easiest way to give lessons is to do so in your own home. The feasibility of this depends upon your available space and the kind of family life that you lead, but if you can use your own home, this is a trouble free way of working. You can set aside an evening or two per week for teaching and you can also run the occasional weekend workshop.

If you can't work from home, look into the possibility of hiring a room at a local pub. They may be happy to let you do this for a very small fee, or even for nothing as long as your students take their break in the pub. Pubs all sell soft drinks and many provide coffee, so there is no need for you or your students to get drunk during their break. A pub that sells food will often be very happy to let you have a room for a day's training as long as your students take their lunch in the pub restaurant. Fortunately "pub grub" is usually very affordable. If you don't live in a country that has the kind of friendly family pubs that we have in the UK, try a restaurant, a sandwich bar with an upstairs room, a hotel or something similar. A local shop may have a back room that you can use.

There are plenty of astrology schools all around the world and there is nothing to prevent you from applying to them to work for them as a teacher. Many of these schools offer work as tutors for postal courses or face-to-face class work. If there is a Tarot or other esoteric organisation around, you can apply to these for teaching jobs. If there is nothing going on, you can always start your own school by setting up a postal course and then advertising it in the esoteric magazines and in your local newspaper.

Adult institutions and regular schools

Adult institutions may be happy to hire you, but some are funny about employing people to teach Tarot or astrology. It is worth enquiring about this because the work and the money are guaranteed even when there are very few students in attendance. All such institutes will ask for verification and qualifications in order to ensure that you know what you are doing. In the UK, you will need basic qualifications, such as the City and Guilds part I and II. The good news is that your local adult institution itself will be able to offer you this course. This kind of qualification is not difficult to obtain, as the course is not long, neither is it arduous and best of all, it is not expensive. In fact, if the institution intends to employ you, it may offer you the course at a reduced price, which makes it even more affordable.

About 12 years ago, Sasha took one of these courses, called an ACSETT course (we can't for the life of us remember what these initials stand for, but we think the A is for adult and the TT is for teacher training.) This course took up one afternoon a week for 13 weeks and at the end of it the class had a small party during which they were all awarded certificates. Sasha was taught to organise single lessons, a term's work (for US readers, a term is a semester) and a whole year's course. This was all done in a hands-on manner by working with others in small groups. The students were all given opportunities to try out different forms of teaching, such as using overhead projectors and various types of demonstration. Sasha found this immensely useful and still organises her teaching along the lines that she learned during this course. This training course cost very little, and Sasha and her classmates had a lot of fun doing it.

The world of commerce

Some firms will spend money on courses or workshops on such things as coping with stress in the workplace, and this kind of subject can cross over into our world. You might just get away with being hired by a commercial organisation to teach Feng Shui for business, but if you want to teach psychic development, Rune reading, the Tarot and so on, you probably won't be able to do so in a business environment.

Job applications

Far-fetched as it may seem, it is possible to pick up work for those who have to sift through job applications. This kind of work suits astrologers, numerologists, graphologists and possibly some types of clairvoyants, as it is usually done at a distance, with only the application form to go on. This is usually done without the knowledge of the applicant. Whether any kind of reading done without the subject of the reading having knowledge of it and consenting to it is ethical, is a very moot point.

Lectures and demonstrations

You can offer to give a talk or a demonstration at your local Spiritualist centre. This work is unpaid (apart from travelling expenses) but it is satisfying, it gets your name around and it brings spin-off work in the form of private sittings. You may be happy to help out by running a development circle, by giving healing and making the tea. None of this will make you a millionaire, but it has its uses, and getting out into pleasant company and having fun with friends makes a nice change.

Dial-a-psychic phone line companies

Sasha's niece, Tracey has worked for one of those dial-a-psychic telephone companies that advertise in the papers. This did not pay well per reading, as compared to giving personal readings, but it suited Tracey's circumstances at the time because she couldn't work from home at that point in her life. Some of the companies employ Readers to work on the phones in the company's premises while others arrange for Readers to receive phone calls at their own homes. As far as we can tell, both methods work well for the Readers and also for their clients.

The firm that employed Tracey gave all their Readers an impressive training course, which was aimed at developing the Reader's psychic ability to a high degree. There are, however, some firms in this field that have a dreadful reputation. Some companies give their Readers a set of printed cards that have the meanings of some of the Tarot cards printed upon them, and all the Reader is required to do is to read out what is printed on these cards. In short, the so called "Readers" who work in these rip-off organisations may have no more idea about Tarot reading than might a lump of cement. Having said that, we have phoned some of the firms that advertise these services at random, and in each case the Reader appeared to be as good as the norm. This is one of those areas that looks suspiciously like a first class rip-off but which may well be perfectly all right. If you fancy working for an organisation of this kind, go and see the people who run the thing, ask to see how the Readers work and use your own intuition as to whether you want to become involved or not.

Lecturing

We have covered this subject pretty thoroughly in other chapters of this book, but there are a few points that are worth taking looking at in a little more detail. The first thing to bear in mind is that lecturing work is usually spasmodic and should only be looked on as a nice change from your usual routine, and of course, an opportunity to hand out cards and leaflets, etc.

Setting fees can be awkward and even we don't always get this right. Try asking the organisation's secretary what the usual situation is and see what you think. If you need time to consider the job, tell the secretary that you will ring him back in a day or so. A small group that uses regular speakers will probably have a set fee, and they should also pay travelling expenses. If the money is poor but the venue is local to your place of work, balance this against the possibility of spin-off clients, but if the venue is miles from your home and the money is poor, turn the job down.

If you are asked to state your price, work out the time you will spend on the whole job, including travelling to and from the venue, and balance this against your hourly rate for readings and charge half. For instance, if you charge £40 or $60 per hour for your readings and you think you will be away from home for four hours, charge about £80 or $120. You may need to charge a lower hourly rate for a whole day's workshop.

If you are asked to take all or part of your fee as a percentage, ensure that the size of the audience, the price that they are being charged and your share of the take will be enough to make the job worthwhile. Finally, if your intuition starts ringing "rip-off" bells, hearken to it!

Broadcasting

Most of us are flattered to be asked to go on the radio and it can be great fun, but it can be a real minefield for the unwary. Be ruthlessly honest with yourself, because if you have a slow speech pattern that is full of deep and meaningful pauses, broadcasting won't work for you. If awkward questions throw you and you can't respond with a fast riposte, then forget it. If you can think on your feet, talk, listen and cope with a dozen things at once, broadcasting can be fun, and these days very few presenters are likely to be "knockers". In the States, there are far more opportunities to get onto a show. There are also various sources available that will give you guidance on how to handle radio and TV interviews, as well as guides to all the various stations and programs. Try your local bookstore (the larger ones can find any book in print, nowadays!). Or, even simpler, get onto the Internet; wherever you live, you can find information on sites such as Dan Poynter's Para Publishing site (web addresses are shown in the addendum at the back of this book).

If you are doing this for the experience or to drum up local business, you may be happy to do it without a fee, but always ask if there is something in the kitty, even if this only covers the costs of your travel and car parking. If there is a fee of any kind at all, be sure that you invoice the company as soon as you can and if you are not paid within a month of doing the show, send a copy invoice and then chase this up.

CONSULTING AS A SIDELINE TO RELATED WORK

The mental & physical health field – spiritual healing – recruitment – banking

In this chapter, we turn the idea of ancillary jobs and look at consulting as an ancillary to something else. You may wish to use astrology, palmistry, clairvoyance, graphology, numerology, Rune or Tarot reading or a whole host of other methods as an attachment to some other kind of work. The following list will show you what we mean:

- Psychology or psychotherapy.
- Complementary medicine, treatments and therapies, hypnotherapy, etc.
- Spiritual healing.
- Recruitment and job applications.
- Banking.

The mental and physical health field

The idea here is that the ability to give an accurate character reading by what we might call "occult" means could be useful in a number of related fields. The validity of this is indisputable but the practical application might be difficult. Those who wish to work in what one could consider a respectable or semi-establishment area such as psychotherapy or osteopathy will find it hard to use such methods openly. Even if it is not possible to offer a reading openly,

being able to read handwriting or to work out someone's character-
istics by numerology or by basic astrology may help the consultant
in a behind-the-scenes manner.

There are plenty of areas where a reading can be offered as part
of the package, either at a separate price or as part of the deal. Healing, aromatherapy, hypnotherapy and many other forms of alternative work require a high level of intuition as part and parcel of the
job, and such skills as clairvoyance or psychometry will be used as
a natural pathway to understanding what is going on inside the patient. Whether this just occurs naturally during the treatment or
whether some kind of reading is offered as a separate issue depends
upon the Therapist, the patient and the circumstances at the time of
the consultation.

Spiritual healing

A spiritual healer is guaranteed to be clairvoyant and probably
an excellent medium into the bargain, and it would be a strange
healing session that didn't include this as part and parcel of the task.
If a healer is also a skilled Reader, he can always hand his patient a
business card that lists his other divinations so that the patient can
consult him for this at another time if he or she wishes to do so.

Recruitment

We actually cover this elsewhere, but there is an unusual "Sasha
story" that can be added to this section. Many years ago I spent
quite a few years working for a recruitment consultancy that hired
engineers to work on large projects overseas. The leaders and supervisors of these projects were important to the success of every
job, and my boss expected me to produce an astrological reading as
part of the recruitment procedure. In less important cases, where we
simply talked to the candidates, I would sit in the room in my guise
of secretary and "gofer", and watch the applicant's hands, reporting
back on anything that seemed relevant.

One day, we were recruiting a low-level supervisor to take charge
of a number of Asian and Oriental "coolies" for a nasty, dirty job in
the Arabian desert. I was unhappy about the man who was being

interviewed, because everything about his hands (and especially the swollen percussion area) shouted to me that this man had no patience and that he would be arrogant and even cruel towards the workers. Nobody cared tuppence about the comfort and happiness of a bunch of Filipino workers, but they did care about having the job done properly without a surly and possibly destructive workforce to deal with - so this man was not taken on.

Banking

Jan was a banker and part of his job was lending out the bank's money. Jan lent money to lots of people for many different purposes and eventually, he supervised others who themselves did the lending, and he had the responsibility for giving a yea or nay to the bigger loans. Did he use his astrological knowledge before dishing out a few million quid to an applicant? What do you think?

Chapter 10

FAIRS AND FESTIVALS

Sheila McGuirk - psychic fairs & festivals - your space is your altar - colour coding - all the fun of the fair

We have decided to give the topic of working at fairs and festivals a chapter to itself because there is quite a lot to take into consideration. There are various kinds of events that you may wish to work at, and the range is quite big, so let us start with the smallest and work our way up.

Advice from Sheila McGuirk

Sheila McGuirk has some advice here for new Readers, which is to offer your services at school fetes, fund-raising fairs or craft fairs, as this is a wonderful way of gaining experience and of building confidence. Sheila says that all such experience is invaluable, as you will not be dealing with your friends and family but with the general public. Despite the fact that they are paying next to nothing for their reading and that all your takings will probably go to charity, the public is as demanding under these circumstances as in any other situation.

Such things as county fairs and horse fairs might be useful, but these might be the province of the local Gypsy community who won't welcome other Readers on their "patch". Local Radio and TV stations and even local newspapers occasionally put on events that you could possibly participate in. The message here is to keep your eyes and ears open and work out what might be worth the effort to do. The marketing spin-off from these events is that you take the opportunity to give your literature and business cards out to a wide range of people. Don't rule out a local flea market.

Psychic fairs and festivals

There are plenty of psychic and mystic type festivals that you can attend and these vary greatly in size and scope. The success or otherwise of these events depends upon the amount of local advertising that the organisers arrange, and also on other imponderables such as the weather and competing events in the locality. I remember one festival in a town called Basildon that was a dead loss because it was held on the same day as a far more popular local county fair. On the other hand, in Britain, the days of the football Cup-Final or the World Cup are good ones to do, as all the menfolk are glued to the television and the women are let off the leash to do what they want. The same is probably the case for the World Series in the USA or something else of the kind.

If you decide to work at a psychic festival, firstly find out the cost of renting space for this event and also the size of the space that will be allocated. Often a table can be used by two Readers, which means that if you can get together with a friend, you can join forces and cut many of your costs. This is even more true if you have to travel to the venue and/or stay overnight somewhere.

At this point, we will give you a list of the kind of things you will need to take with you to any psychic festival, and you might wish to make several photocopies of this to keep as a checklist. Don't forget to add anything else that you specifically might need:-

- A vehicle to take you and all your baggage to and from the event.
- A small table in addition to the space that you rent.
- A comfortable folding chair to keep in the car, in case the ones supplied are "backbreakers". A comfortable cushion to sit on.
- Scissors, string, pens, pencils, an eraser, a ruler, a hammer, a knife, a screwdriver, drawing pins, tacks, stick tape, sticky stuff, paper, folders, pieces of card, a small picture frame for

your prices or other information, and a picture hook to hang it from.

- A tape-recorder, tapes and an extension lead with a four-plug adapter.
- A lamp or two.
- Curtains or cloths to hang around a stand or to spread on the table.
- A couple of flasks of hot water for tea and coffee.
- Tea, coffee, sugar, paper towels, travel wipes, a spoon, a knife, sandwiches, fruit, cans of soft drink or bottled water.
- In winter, a small electric heater could prove very useful.
- Tools such as your Tarot cards, crystal ball, runes etc.
- If you are an astrologer, take a laptop computer, a printer, a long extension lead and plenty of adapters, a spare ink cartridge and paper for your printer.
- A box for change and a float (notes and coins).
- Lots of business cards and leaflets or brochures.
- A change of clothes, especially if the weather or conditions are changeable or if you intend to be away overnight.
- Toothbrush and toothpaste, deodorant; a razor if you're a man.
- Aspirins, indigestion tablets, plasters, any special medicines.
- Don't forget to take tampons, pads and spare underwear if necessary.

Your space is your altar

We remember our friend, Eve Bingham, once telling me that a Reader's table or working space is his or her altar. To those who don't work on a highly spiritual vibration this notion may appear a little far-fetched, but if you look at the concept for a moment or two you will see that there is truth in the idea. There is always a spiritual element in consulting work, so why not have something around you that you feel links you to the spirit world, a talisman or statuette of some kind, or even just something that makes you feel happy.

Colour coding

A chat to our friend, Sue Lilly, brought up some interesting points about the colour and style in which you decorate your working area. If you work as part of an organisation such as BAPS at a major festival, you have no choice but to abide by their rules and regulations. Your table will be of a standard size and the colour scheme of the festival will dictate the colour of the cloth that is on your table. However, if you are working at a less formal occasion, the decor of your stand, space or table is a very personal matter. At some festivals you will have a proper stand that looks like a booth. Some of these spaces are larger than others so you need to take enough material with you to cover any size and shape of booth. Creating something attractive and personal can be great fun, especially if you happen to be good at window dressing. If you only have a table, this too can be covered with an attractive cloth and any ornaments or bits and pieces that you wish to have around you.

Sue said that she has noticed over the years that the style and the colours that Readers choose for their stand reflect the personal style of the Readers themselves. Furthermore, that the colour scheme actually attracts the type of people to the stand that are drawn towards the style and personality of the Readers on that stand. For example, one lovely pair of our friends called Dot and Reg, used to work the festivals under the title of "The House of Avalon". Theirs was a Wiccan organisation. Sometimes they worked as a pair and at other times they came "mob-handed" as we Londoners say, bringing other Readers with them to take a large stand and to work as a team. These kindly and fun-filled folk always dressed their space beautifully in dramatic red and black, and they gave their stand and themselves a slight "occult" appearance. Customers who enjoyed that kind of atmosphere went straight to them for their readings, and there must have been plenty of them, because unless the festival itself was a complete turkey, Dot and Reg were never short of work.

Sue, being a healer by profession in addition to her astrological and clairvoyant work, says that she prefers to be surrounded by green, the colour of the heart chakra. Many other healers use pale blue or turquoise, the colours associated with the throat chakra which represents communication and other forms of healing.

I can't remember ever giving colour a thought when I worked at the festivals, but the moment that Sue started talking about colour I realised that I always chose a bright golden yellow. Indeed, even now when I give short readings in bookstores to promote my books, I always take a sunny yellow cloth with me to put on whatever table the shop gives me to work on. In esoteric work, yellow is especially associated with teaching and writing. I have always wondered why so many of the people who come to me for readings at such festivals are themselves interested in writing, teaching, acting, broadcasting, dancing, painting and performing. Now I know!

A chat to a lovely friend of ours called Dave Bingham, reminded me that our other friends Renee Hindle and Betty Nugent always dressed their space with loads of pretty paper and silk flowers in pastel shades. Another friend called Gordon Smith kept a small group of Buddha statuettes on his table, while one or two of the more greedy Readers surrounded themselves with piles of gizmos that they hoped to sell. So much so in one memorable case that it was almost impossible to see the Reader peering out from the midst of all the clutter. Dave commented that like himself, I only ever kept the tools of my trade on my table, these being my books of astrological tables (in later years I swapped these for a laptop computer), a box of Tarot cards and a good lamp to read hands by. Along with a really small tape-recorder, that was always more than enough for me. Dave is a sand reader and as such he needed his bowl of sand and also his Tarot cards and a good light. Dave's comment was that we are both the type of Reader who calls a spade a spade and not a shovel, and we attracted those clients who appreciated a straightforward approach.

All the fun of the fair

Such fairs can be great fun, as you will work alongside other Readers and during the course of the event you will pick up a good many tips from the old hands. Some festivals have a wonderful atmosphere where everybody has a terrific time, but others seem to encourage jealousy and irritating behaviour from some of the participants. Much of the atmosphere at these events is linked to their success, and it is a fact that if all the stand holders make money everybody is happy, but if the event is a damp squib, tempers will fray. Look into your ephemeris or your crystal ball and have a word with your Spiritual guides before spending money on booking the space for such an event, and try to work out whether it will be worth the considerable effort of doing it or not.

(What other western business book would suggest that you consult a crystal ball or ephemeris before embarking on a new venture?)

START-UP COSTS

The expensive divinations – other expenses – the Internet – teaching – raising money for start-up costs

Even if you only intend to work from home on a part-time basis, there will be a few expenses to plan for. You don't have to buy everything that you need in one go, because you can often gradually equip yourself as time goes by. If Christmas is coming or if your birthday is looming, consider asking your friends and relatives for some of the things that you will need.

Do remember to keep all receipts that relate to your business and if you can get your mom and dad or other generous relatives to buy you a large item such as a tape-recorder or an answering machine - so much the better! The following list of items will give you an idea of what you might need:

Items that are related specifically to readings
- A table and a fancy cloth to go over it.
- A crystal ball, Tarot cards, Runes, dowsing rods or any other tool of the trade.
- A telephone and an answering machine. If you work from a friend's house, you will need to make some kind of arrangements regarding what proportion of their phone bill belongs to you. Itemised bills are the answer to this one. Remember to claim the costs against income tax. A mobile/cell phone is also useful in this case.
- A tape recorder and tapes.

- If you are a palmist you will need a good light and the equipment for taking hand prints.
- If you are an astrologer, you can do charts by hand, but this is so much better on a computer and printer that sooner or later you will have to buy these.
- You may want candles, music tapes and CDs, incense sticks, a vase or two and a pot-plant. Try to put as many of these items as possible against tax.

Items that don't relate specifically to readings
- Business cards and leaflets.
- Stationery and some form of letterhead.
- A ton of odds and ends such as a stapler, paperclips, elastic bands, bulldog-clips, rulers, different kinds of sticky stuff and glue, pens, pencils, note-pads and a calculator.
- A diary and an address book.
- Local and more distant phone books.
- A picture frame in which to display a certificate of competence if you have one.
- Books, audio-tapes and videos on your subjects.

You are bound to buy books and you may attend lessons, talks or a group and this will be an on-going expense that can also be put against tax.

If you are a beginner and wish to do Tarot readings, you will want a set of Tarot cards. We suggest that you start with a Ryder-Waite pack or one of its clones at the outset. This is a very precise and clear pack, which will get you well-grounded. Many people find after a few months that they have a preference for one of the dozens of other types of Tarot packs and that's fine. Use the deck that you find suits you and your style best.

You can buy Tarot cards in most main larger towns, ask around. A good shop will have a range of decks, so you can look before you buy. If you're in or near London, an excellent range of decks can be found at Mysteries (address at the back of this book). If you live elsewhere and have a problem in obtaining a deck, try the Internet (as usual... as we said before, you can find practically anything on the 'Net). The benefit is that you will be able to look at the cards on the screen before you buy them, which you often can't do in shops.

The expensive divinations

Astrologers are in a different ball-park to other Readers because a modern astrologer's equipment is expensive. A computer and software will cost money, but with a bit of luck this will soon start to pay for itself. Consider all the uses that you and your family might have for a computer, and take your time about choosing what you want. Get advice if you don't know enough about computers. If you are only thinking about your own needs and if these needs only run to astrology and a bit of word-processing plus a simple spreadsheet or two, you don't need top dollar equipment. If you or your family have other needs, then get the best you can, so that you have enough memory and disc space for everything that is required.

If you buy a computer second hand from a friend, make sure that you know exactly what condition it is in and whether it is worth the money. Computers become outdated and lose their resale value very quickly. If a friend or relative offers to give you a computer, then walk a fine line between not looking a gift-horse in the mouth and not landing yourself with a piece of useless junk - especially in view of the fact that you will be expected to be eternally grateful! The problems are likely to lie with the software situation, because if the machine has come out of the ark, or if it is a home-built contraption, it may be impossible to obtain any astrology software that will run on it.

Even those of you who are not astrologers, if you are into computers, you can buy software for the Tarot, the Runes, for graphology, Chinese astrology and numerology. If you are an astrologer, you might wish to buy software that produces astrological reports that you can sell. If you only want the software to produce charts without any reports, you can restrict yourself to this. Jan and I use the Solar Fire packages for charts of various kinds.

If you look at the appendix at the back of this book you will see the listing for the British (including worldwide) Astrology year book, and this shows various firms that advertise specialist software. If you are in the USA or elsewhere, you will need to look up such a book or a specialist magazine like The Mountain Astrologer, to find your local astrology centres, and then you can get in touch with other astrologers and ask what kind of software they use. Sooner or later you will find just the right thing for you, because you may be more comfortable with one program than another.

Other expenses

Even if you are not an astrologer, you may want to type, write or otherwise communicate on paper, so you will need something with which to do this. You may buy decent note paper and envelopes (put these on your birthday-present list). You may decide that you need a computer anyway. If you only need a wordprocessor, take a look at today's typewriters, as these have most of the word-processing features for a tenth of the price of a new computer.

If you do get a computer mainly for charts, etc. then you don't need the most expensive wordprocessor and spreadsheet programs; most day-to-day requirements can be done on any one of the cheaper programs than abound, especially in the Freeware / Shareware markets Look in PC magazines, or (you'd never guess where...) the Internet!

Some good programs even come free of charge attached to PC magazines. We've seen freebie copies of Lotus ® WordPro and Lotus ® 123 on PC magazine covers, and these are full-blown professional programs! Sure, the versions are a bit out of date, but any version of anything to do with computers is out of date in no time at all anyway. One just can't keep up with the rate of progress in this arena, so one gets used to skipping a couple of versions in any event. So, the word is don't go lashing out unnecessarily, investigate properly first.

The Internet

We talk about the Internet so often in this book, and we use it (or "surf" it) so frequently that it's as well to say, very clearly, that this has become one of the most useful sources of information and means of communication in the last few years that one can imagine.

We find it amusing that a few days ago, we looked up the brand new Bertelsmann on-line bookshop, and found this very book - Prophecy for Profit - already listed there, at 10% discount, for de-

---

Jan's Stories... *(just for a change)*

One of Sasha's friends who isn't yet "Inter-mechanised" has frequently asked me to look up esoteric bits of research for him, for articles / books he writes. I've found in-depth information for him and for us, on such things as "the Voodoo Queen of New Orleans", Saint Malachi, the complexities of Mayan and Aztec calendars / astrological beliefs, Hitler's (alleged) astrologer, latest reports on ancient Egyptian archaeological discoveries, and a multitude of other valuable information - sometimes within a few minutes!. I can read the news headlines in South Africa whilst writing this piece, and I checked the weather on the Costa del Sol recently, just before we took a short holiday there.

---

livery in 2 - 4 weeks! We'd better get moving with finishing off this book very quickly if we're to meet that deadline!

On the communication front, we recently queried a US organisation by e-mail about some correspondence that was overdue. We had an e-mail reply within half a day, and when their letter arrived, it had done a side trip via Denmark somehow, even though it was correctly addressed, and had taken a couple of weeks to reach us.

This evening, Sasha had an e-mail request (or she-mail as she calls it) for some information needed in the States. We happened to pick it up within minutes of its despatch, and if we hadn't been otherwise tied up, we could have responded within ten minutes.

If we wish, we can send this whole book, ready for printing, to an American printer over the Internet, and receive a substantial discount for thus letting them have a "troublefree" order; i.e. an electronic file that essentially they need do no more than load into their equipment and churn out thousands of books.

None of this was feasible just a few years ago, so we seriously recommend that you give consideration to what uses you could put the Internet to for yourself.

Teaching

If you wish to teach or lecture you might need any of the following items:-

- A white board and/or flip charts, white-board markers and a cloth for cleaning the board.
- An overhead projector, transparencies and overhead transparency pens. Even if you don't have your own projector, you will need to prepare transparencies for lectures at places where they have a projector available.
- Photocopied material to hand out.
- An extension lead and perhaps an extra light.
- Possibly a cassette recorder and/or special tapes to play during your demonstrations.
- Transport.
- Business cards and leaflets.

Raising money for start-up costs

As businesses go, ours takes very little to start up. Other kinds of business might need premises and office equipment, a shop, stock, a particular kind of vehicle, staff, large amounts of stationery and letterhead, and much else. As a Reader, you may only need a phone and somewhere for you and your client to sit; that is the upside of our work, but the downside comes when you try to raise money through usual business sources. However, you may decide that you need a car or a computer or other fairly expensive items. We will look at your needs in detail a little later, but in this chapter we will consider some ways of raising money for your start-up costs.

Raising money

In practically any kind of business, you can take a business plan and proposed cashflow projection to a bank or any other financial institution, and you might get a loan out of them if you are lucky. If you tell your bank manager that you are starting up as a "fortune-teller", well... in short, they just won't want to know. They want a track record, security, a business plan and any number of other things. What they mostly don't tell you is this: they are primarily looking at making their lending safe, and your side of things takes second place.

Let's have a look at this matter of capital and working capital.

Capital can be thought of as the money *you* invest in your business. This is a *long-term* need.

Working capital is the money used for day-to-day running of the business. It is money that is used for *short-term* requirements, like covering you while you are awaiting payment for your services. As you will be getting paid by your clients on the spot at each reading, your working capital needs should be low. This is important - you can not afford to let people pay you "at the end of the month", etc. You *must* work on a "cash-on-delivery" (C.O.D.) basis.

Overdraft facility. If you do have a good bank manager, he will tell you that your *capital need* (the money you want for setting up purposes), is not the right purpose for an overdraft/bank loan. That, believe me, (this is Jan writing here, if you hadn't guessed) is sound advice, even if it isn't solving your problem. An overdraft facility is only meant for short-term bridging finance - to cover you if *money already owed to you* is delayed in getting paid. You may well be able to get an overdraft facility or a bank loan if you provide enough security, but be aware that you are then taking responsibility for the facility and its repayment on your own, because if it isn't repaid as arranged, the bank will just "call up" the overdraft and realise whatever security you pledged or committed to the bank. A bank loan is usually repaid by fixed instalments on a monthly basis.

So, what do you do?

First of all, you need to have enough *capital* to get your business off the ground. If you don't have it, the business will crash. You can raise capital from your savings, from selling something (that motor bike, or that old caravan that you use once in a blue moon, etc.). Keep in mind that *an overdraft or borrowed money are not sources of capital!* You could, however, borrow money on an *indefinite* basis from your parents, spouse, or any other generous relative. If you borrow from a friend, you can be sure that they will want it back at the most inconvenient time. Work out how much you will need, and *don't* use it for a flashy new car, new clothes or the biggest and best computer in town. Use it for your business cards, your stationery, the equipment you really need, and if relevant, use it for a basic computer. You can now get a brand new computer and printer that will do everything you really need, for as little as £500 ($800). Second-hand, for much less.

You may have to save up for a while, and that's well worth the wait. You don't have to get everything you need all at the same time either, so get things as you go along. Just find the *capital* you need without borrowing it.

Secondly, your working capital needs; these should not be that high, (you are selling a service, not stock), and they should build up from putting aside a portion of the reading income that you make. At the outset you might well be short, and here you can do a bit of borrowing, sensibly. If you have a life assurance policy that has been going for a few years, you may be able to use it as security for an overdraft / bank loan. An even better idea would be to approach the insurance company for a loan from them. This will normally be available for as long as you like, whereas a bank will want to see regular reductions in your borrowing. A loan from the insurance company would be a *medium-term* loan, which is far more appropriate for your needs, just in case you have delays in building up your practice. You can expect your practice to take at least six months, often longer, before it will bring in a reasonable and regular income.

If you go this route, then make sure you commit yourself to start repaying the loan *as soon as you possibly can*, because the life insurance is a valuable investment that should not be played around with for any length of time.

There are other forms of finance, but these vary widely from country to country. The best thing to do is to talk to an accountant or your bank manager. They will be best placed to advise you on local sources of finance and their merits or otherwise for your specific needs.

Finally, one word on another tempting source of borrowing; you could probably increase the mortgage on your house to get some money for the business. The word of advice I have for you is: **Don't!** I won't list all the reasons, why, just take my word for it that after over 30 years in banking and lending money in all sorts of ways, I strongly advise you not to mess around with the roof over your (and your family's) heads. `nuff said.

Having said that, there are small business schemes around that might be worth investigating, and in some cases if you can prove that you have a figure such as £1,000 in cash to back yourself with, such an institution might lend you a further £1,000. Depending upon your personal circumstances, you are quite likely to be able to raise a loan for a car or a computer, as these are tangible things that banks are more likely to lend money on. In other cases, you may even be able to raise money for a holiday... and then use this for your business. This is not the right thing to do, but sometimes it might be worth thinking about. You must bear in mind that any money you borrow has to be paid back, and with interest, so finding these repayments has to become part of your weekly or monthly budget requirements. Check a couple of institutions for better interest rates.

If you have a relative or a friend who can lend you something to start up with that is a better option, as they are unlikely to add interest to the loan, but do be scrupulous about paying them back. Do this on a weekly or monthly basis rather than trying to save the whole amount in one go, because you will find it easier to pay off the loan in this way. Don't let your sponsor down... they may not say anything about it, but they won't forget. Anyway, if you are absolutely scrupulous about repaying your loan, you may be able to go back to them for another one at a later date if necessary.

Chapter 12

WHAT SHOULD YOU CHARGE FOR A READING?

Rip-off merchants – high, low & realistic fees – a high-income area – three ways of costing your readings – don't shoot yourself in the foot – other considerations – hidden costs – facts to remember – time is money – value for value – comparisons are odious – charlatanism –fraudulent mediums – clients' expectations – off days – off lives – disastrous Readers

A tiny minority of Readers charge the earth for a reading, an even smaller minority set out to rip clients off. A great many charge far too little, while the vast majority simply don't charge enough! So let us take a brief look at all these scenarios for just a moment.

Rip-off merchants

There is a well-known rip-off technique in which a Reader tells a client that she or some member of her family is due to be ill and that the Reader will perform some magical trick to avert this disaster. If the client falls for this one, he or she will certainly find herself forking out a great deal of money for this dubious "service". This ploy works well in third world countries where such confidence tricksters can prey on the ignorance of their clientele, but it doesn't really work in the first world. We have only come across two such persons who were known to have done this in the UK, but we have heard many such stories about Readers in India and Africa.

High fees

There are always stories going round about "some woman over in Anytown who charges £120/$300 for a reading", but we never actually seem to come across this mysterious woman. One group of consultants who apparently charge a great deal of money for readings are some of the so-called top astrologers who are the heads of this or that organisation. The fact is that these people don't rely upon readings for their living and so their charges are probably meant to be off-putting. There are also grounds for the view that with the amount of experience, research, time and money that top people have put into their jobs, a very high charge is not inequitable. The same applies to, for example, a Harley Street medical specialist. However, most Readers don't fall into this category and we will be looking at the question of charging as it applies to the majority of Readers.

There was a well-known Reader around in London in years gone by, who routinely charged a great deal for his readings. This chap had a regular spot on a popular radio station and also a consultancy in a very smart area of London. The readings must have been worth the high fees that were charged or he wouldn't have remained in business. He is no longer liv-

> **Sasha's stories...**
>
> Jan doesn't give many readings as he prefers the research side of our work, but I do still give the occasional reading. I trade on the fact that my name is known and respected, I have full confidence in my abilities, built up over many years, so therefore I charge a higher than average amount - but still not a ridiculous one. If I needed to rely upon readings for an income, I would lower my prices so as to attract a larger clientele, but I restrict the number of readings because they have to fit into my busy writing and publishing schedule. Jan tells me that at least one on-line bookshop (mentioned in another chapter as well...) is already advertising this book for sale with a 2 -4 week delivery time, so you can see what pressures we live with!

ing in London - perhaps he retired to live on a yacht!

Low fees

Those who charge very little may be just setting out as Consultants and they may not yet be sure enough of their skills to charge a realistic amount. This is fair enough, as it gives the fledgling Reader a feeling that even if the reading is not all that wonderful, he or she hasn't taken much money for it. If you are a beginner, you will probably be best to stick to a nominal fee until you are really comfortable with your skills. There are some who charge very little because they wish to give a service to the public rather than to consider making a living from their readings. This is fair enough. A Reader is perfectly entitled to charge very little for his skills or even to give them away for nothing if he or she chooses to do so.

Realistic fees

All of us are unsure of our abilities to a greater or lesser extent, and this uncertainty is due to the fact that we often work alone and therefore have no benchmark to measure ourselves against. In most proper jobs, there is a scale of wages, salaries and consultancy fees that is par for the job in question. There are usually also performance criteria against which to measure oneself. It can sometimes be difficult for a Consultant in a far more ordinary field than ours to get his fee structure right, but for us it can be almost impossible. Very few Readers have the kind of self-belief that allows them to set a high price for their services and then to defend it by telling enquirers how good they are. However, there are ways of finding the right price to charge (more or less), so now let us look at the knotty problem of the right fee for the job.

A high income area

If you live and work in an area where the people around you have very little money to spend, you can't charge high fees, while if you work in a posh area where the public have money to burn you can charge considerably more. It also follows that rentals and other costs in a posh area tend to be far higher than elsewhere, so fees have to reflect such factors. It is possible to work in a high income area, even if you can't afford to live in one, as long as you are prepared to travel and to work away from your home some of the time.

In the UK there are a few alternative health centres in smart areas of London which will allow a Consultant to rent a room on a daily basis. The rental for such a room is expensive, as is the use of the reception and booking facilities, but such a place provides a clientele who will happily pay a high fee for consultations. As long as there is a good throughput of business, it will make the expense worthwhile. It may not be possible to rent the space for more than one or two days a week. When one considers the fact that you will have to get to the venue and spend a day away from home, and also the amount of potential business that you might have there, one or two days per week are probably plenty.

If like most of us, you can't take a room in Kensington or Wimpole Street, you will need to tailor your prices to your local scene. Just like any plumber, electrician or other workman, you should try to discover what other Consultants charge in your area, as this will give you the best idea of the going rate for the job. Go for a reading yourself to find out. The reading may be useful in any event. If you still have no real idea, here are three ways of assessing your situation. It is interesting to note that each one of these has been arrived at by a different person, whose outlook and thought processes are very different from each of the other two, but the interesting thing is that we have all come up with more or less the same kind of hourly rate.

Before we go over our method of pricing readings, remember that the kind of price scale that we are suggesting is for city areas where there is a reasonably high level of income. You may wish to look through the ideas that we offer and then still tailor your prices up or down from those that we suggest. Even half the amount that we suggest can be reasonable, especially if your readings are not your main form of income.

If you are flat broke and keen to build a clientele, then half our amount will get you a fair number of clients and enough income to keep the wolf from the door. It all really depends upon your personal circumstances. Our view is that once you have a reasonable clientele of about ten to twenty clients per week, and when you are completely comfortable with your skills, you should gradually move your prices up to something in the area that we are suggesting.

Three ways of costing your readings

The following methods of costing out readings are worked out in British currency (Pounds) only. We have not given the usual approximate US Dollar conversions for the simple reason that the amounts involved are, in these examples, very specific to the country in which you live.

For example, when we talk about the cost of a meal for two in a nice restaurant, this can be very different to just a straight conversion of one currency to another; a figure of £40 would be typical in the UK, but in South Africa the equivalent (400 Rand) would feed at least four people in an equivalent restaurant!

The Sasha Fenton method

One way that I have always judged the cost of a reading is by the cost of a make-over at the local beauty parlour! This may sound nuts, but the majority of clients are women, and if a woman is prepared to spend a certain amount to have her hair coloured or permed and her face sorted out once in a while, she will be prepared to spend about the same on our services. In London, an hour and a half session in a high-street hairdresser's establishment will cost between £50 and £70, depending upon where the shop is and what exactly the client has done. Therefore a good middling hourly price for an hour's reading is probably around £40 to £45. Apply the same comparative reasoning in the country and area where you live.

The Jonathan Dee method

Jon bases his reading price on the cost of a meal for two, plus drinks, in a nice restaurant. The kind of restaurant that Jon describes is neither a top-person's overpriced haunt, nor a trucker's burger bar. Something like a good Chinese or Italian restaurant would do. Jon suggests that you take a friend out for a meal to see what it comes to; this being purely for research purposes, of course! Jonathan estimates that such an evening out would cost him about £40 or more (including the tip). In the chapter on taxation, you will see that you can set such an expense against your tax bill, so do be sure to keep the restaurant receipt.

The Jan Budkowski method

In case you haven't picked up the fact that Jan spent 31 years in banking before giving it all up to publish books, (*Jan:* I gave it all up to be with you, *my skat* [affectionate Afrikaans term]; that's more romantic...) you will soon see the difference in thinking between such long term flakes as Jonathan and me, and the more serious mind-set of the corporate man! So now, over to Jan...

Thanks, Sasha.

This is a slightly longer method and I'll keep it simple, but as Nedbank's motto used to be: If you're Serious about Money...

1. Consider what you need to earn per year, in order to live comfortably and also to make provision for a reasonable pension as well as periodic major expenses, such as changing your car every few years, or buying a new computer; perhaps putting your children through school and/or university; also, to cover the times when you may need to have breaks from work.

Typically, a reasonable figure would be about one and a half times the average annual earnings in whichever country you live. (Remember that as a self-employed person, you don't have the pension schemes and other perks that a salaried person takes for granted). The average salary in the UK is currently close to £20,000 per annum, and our information indicates that a level of about $30,000 per annum is the current figure for the USA. Other countries will have their own levels, and Government Statistical Departments will usually have the details.

Add half of this figure, to allow for savings / pension / other provisions outlined above: e.g. £20,000 + £10,000 = £30,000.

This is now the level of income to aim for. We'll call this amount "A".

Tip:
These calculations can be done very accurately, but for this book, a simpler guide will give a good estimate. Please, however, always do one important thing: do this exercise and all other financial calculations on paper, with a calculator next to you. No matter who you are, mental calculations produce mistakes, and things get left out.

Write your own amount in here: My A = _____

2. Work out how many actual working days you have in a typical year of 365 days. For example, deduct 21 days leave, 12 days for illness and other unforeseen events, about 8 days for public holidays, and weekends (about 8 days per month, thus 104 days in a year).

In this example, deduct (21 + 12 + 8 + 104 = 145) from 365, giving you a total of 220 working days in a typical year. Be conservative and knock this down to 200 days. Right, let's call this figure "B".

Write your figure in here: My B = _____

3. Estimate conservatively the a *average* number of clients you will see per working day, during a whole year. Allow for "dead" periods such as school holidays and the Christmas period.

The number will be substantially less than the number of clients you *can* handle in a day. It will very likely be about 4, at the very best, 5. Being conservative, say 4. We'll call this number "C".

Write your number here: My C = _____

Right, hang in, we're nearly there. Check your own figures again, just to make certain you've got it all right. You are now coming up to a very useful formula that will give you a pretty accurate estimate of what you need to charge for your readings, in order to give you a comfortable income that will provide for your old age as well as other major expenses. One thing that the formula doesn't take into account is income tax. In an estimate like this one, the vast differences in taxation that may apply to you, can't easily be included. You can either do that bit of calculation yourself, or get someone to help out with it. In real life, one finds that other sidelines develop in time that improve on your earnings, or there are a spouse's earnings that help to make up the required total income your family unit needs.

OK, here's the formula, and I'll go through it with you...

A divided by B, divided by C = the charge needed per client reading.

Using my figures as worked out above, this comes out as follows:

A (30,000) divided by B (200) = 150 (i.e. leaving off the decimals for simplicity).

150 divided by C (4) = £37.50

In this example, the result means that you would need to charge £37.50 per reading in order to earn about £30,000 per annum. If you don't live in the UK, just substitute your own currency symbol instead of pounds (£).

Write down your own example using your figures,
A (_____) divided by B(_____) = _____

divide this result by C (_____) = £_____ per reading.

This figure, if you become good enough to charge it per reading, will give a comfortable income if you do your job consistently and apply yourself daily, as you would have to anyway, in a "proper job".

In the UK, a good Reader with a sound reputation and a built up client base should be well able to exceed the figure of £37.50 per reading. So the potential is there, it is up to you to put your mind to it and apply the various ideas and principles outlined in this book.

OK, Sasha, back to you again...

Don't shoot yourself in the foot

While researching this book, we have discovered that despite the usual comments about "some women over the other side of town who is charging a fortune," the majority of Readers charge less than the modest figures that we have suggested. Half of what we suggest as being a reasonable charge for a reading is not unusual even in London, but the reality is that despite the fact that this kind of fee may ensure a good throughput of clients, it is slave labour and it doesn't constitute a living wage. There appear to be a number of reasons for Readers to charge ridiculously low fees and they are as follows:

Readers may fear that their trade will fall away if they increase their prices.

Readers may feel that they don't deserve to charge more or to earn more.

Readers fear that their friends and colleagues who don't charge as much will become envious, critical and even spiteful, and that they will lose these "friends" as a result.

Let us now address each of these points in turn.

As we tell you elsewhere in this chapter, there is a right price for your work that is lurking somewhere, and which you will have to find. If you hike your prices much too high for your area, trade will drop right off, but it is still worth raising your prices to the kind of ball-park figure that we have suggested - even as a kind of pilot scheme - just to see what happens. We think you will be pleasantly surprised by the results. Sure, a few free-loaders will be put off by your price increase, but genuine clients will still come and they will recommend you to their friends.

Many Readers, even those with long years of experience are frightened to charge a proper fee and they don't seem to have the confidence to ask for what is their due. Remember, that as long as you are good at your job and secure in your skills, there is no need for you to give your work away for a pittance. You deserve to be properly paid for what you do. If you worked in a normal job for someone else you would expect to be properly paid, so why not be a good employer as well as a good employee and pay yourself properly?

If your friends can't bear to see you earning a good living from your work, they aren't your friends.

Sasha's summary

So now you have the benefit of the advice of a skilled and experienced corporate executive as well as two long-term Consultants. We have quoted our figures in Sterling and according to the kind of rates that apply at the time of writing in the general London area. However, you must work out what your local scene is, as this may be very different, but the point of this is that the ratio is still the same, whether you are operating in Arizona or the Amazon basin.

Other considerations

You may decide to charge for your time, for instance charging less for a Tarot or Rune reading than for a long-winded job such as mediumship, astrology or a combination of skills in one reading. Alternatively, you may charge for your divination. This means charging less for a fairly easy one like the Tarot and more for a very complicated job, such as graphology. If you offer a variety of divinations, you may decide to charge more for one than for another. There are pros and cons to this because you may find that you have booked a client in for a supposedly simple procedure, only to find that this isn't the right one for the situation. Our feeling is that once you have agreed a fee with your client, you must stick to it even if you take a loss by doing so.

Once in a while, a reading will take more time than you had anticipated or it will require a more complicated divination than you had anticipated; either way it is best to keep to the fee that you agreed with your client in the first place. If you can't spare the time to finish the reading in a way that you are happy with, offer to give the client another session at no charge. There are times when it is far better to look after a client's interests than to appear greedy. If the client is so happy with you after the event that she offers to pay you something extra, please feel free to take this as it is the client's way of thanking you.

Hidden costs

Bear in mind that the money you earn from your readings is not free and clear. If your readings are anything other than an occasional affair, you will have to pay income tax and National Insurance (Social Security) out of this. Your clients may initially contact you by phone but if they leave a message on your answering machine or if you have to change the date of an appointment, you will be making the call. Administration, travel, rental of space, marketing and equipment all have to be paid for. As you will see elsewhere in this book, there could be far more hidden expense than you have accounted for. If you consider that out of every £100 or $100 that you earn, at least 25 per cent goes in tax and perhaps as much as another 20 per cent goes in hidden expenses, you are already down by almost half. So try to find the happy medium between charging so much that you frighten your clients off and charging so little that you are working yourself into the ground or making a loss - then you yourself will be a happy medium!

Some facts to remember

Many clients will have an idea of what a fair price for a reading should be. If they don't at first, they will, sooner or later.

If you are a good Reader and if your charges are too low, your clients themselves will suggest that you should charge more. When this happens, consider increasing your prices.

Some clients will have a totally unrealistic expectation of your fees. For example, if a client last consulted a Reader on the end of Brighton Pier in 1937 and paid half-a-crown (12.5 pence) for the reading, she will be surprised to find that you want more.

If you decide to increase your prices, make the decision a couple of months ahead and then set a definite date for your increase. Perhaps you could review your prices twice a year (once a year at the very least), and then make up your mind whether you want to put them up or leave them as they are for the time being. Inflation reduces the value of money, so charges do need to go up every so often.

> The laws of supply and demand will ensure that if you charge ridiculous fees, you won't get many clients.

> The laws of supply and demand suggest that if you charge lower fees, you could be inundated with clients.

> Regarding the previous point, the laws of human nature suggest to your clients that if you charge peanuts, you must be a lousy Reader (or a monkey)!

> The laws of Murphy suggest that you will never ever get any of this right but that if you are more or less right, it will *feel* right to you - and to your clients.

Time is money

You must set both the price and the time that the reading is likely to take when your client makes the initial enquiry.

If you can group your clients together in one batch, then the majority of them can't overstay their time limit but if you choose to spend more than the allotted time with a client, that is your business.

After a particularly helpful reading, some clients will offer you more money than you have quoted and you should always accept this, as this is the client's way of thanking you.

If a regular client brings you flowers or gives you a little present, accept this gracefully, it is lovely when this happens.

Value for value

Always, give good value for money. You don't need to sit with a client for hours on end and you don't need to sort out every area of their lives, but you do need to give a good reading in whatever time it takes you. This book is all about professionalism. This is your job

Tips

Always give your reading first and then allow the client to pay you afterwards.

If a client gives you the money before you start, then leave it lying openly on your table and only pick it up and put it away when the work is done.

If a reading fails (and believe me this can happen to the best of us), then you must not take money from your client.

If more than the very occasional reading fails, reconsider your skills, your approach or whether you need to take a break from this kind of work and come back to it after a rest or a change of scene.

Even if you are absolutely brilliant, you can't please every client or tell every client what they want to hear. You simply have to accept this fact.

and you are worthy of being treated decently and of being properly paid for what you do. However, greed and short-changing the public has no place in spiritual work.

Comparisons are odious

We all work in different ways, and if you try to copy the style of some other reader you won't be comfortable. Don't fall into the trap of thinking that anyone else is better at the job than you are. We all work in different ways and while someone else may be good at one aspect of the job, you may be better at another. If what you do works for you, that is all that matters.

Charlatanism

We sometimes hear civilians comment that our profession is full of charlatans. If we then ask the accuser to name them so that we can check them out, few names if any, actually emerge. The problem can be one of perception and it tends to arise among those who don't actually visit Readers themselves, but who make this assumption. True charlatans don't last long in this game.

Charlatanism or disappointment?

Some clients will find a reading disappointing because their expectations are too high. Many clients want to hear something specific, such as an assurance of winning a large sum on a lottery or finding a rich husband within the next three months. Other clients simply go for the wrong kind of reading. For instance, a client may go to a palmist or an astrologer who gives them a wonderful overview of their character as well as some of the future events of their lives, when what they really need is a medium who can get through to their late Aunty Fanny. A medium is not a fortune-teller and neither is a graphologist, but some clients don't understand the difference, and somehow their mistake becomes the fault of the Reader.

Some beginners go plunging into the Consultancy game without enough skill or experience behind them and these too can be daubed with the charlatan title. The good news is that, in time, the Reader can only get better, but he or she will need to be open about any lack of experience in order not to land up with a permanently bad reputation.

Fraudulent mediums

The old days of fraudulent mediums who had a whole baggage of tricks to make their clients believe that ghosts and spirits were moaning, wailing and levitating stuff around their rooms have gone. These days, the ordinary public is far too well informed about the stunts that can be performed in films and television to believe the old hocus-pocus that such an old-time fraud might have tried to pull on them. They have seen too many episodes of the X Files to believe in such crap. If you really and truly feel that you have a vocation as a confidence trickster, try something easier than our profession. It is hard enough to do it for real without also having to turn yourself into a stage magician as well!

Clients' expectations

There will always be people you can't please, and you have to accept this as part of the job. If someone is truly dissatisfied with your services, whether they have true cause to be or not, don't take their money, and get them (and their negativity) out of your workplace as swiftly as possible. There are clients who are determined to get a reading for nothing, but this kind of trick is far more common at Mind, Body and Spirit festivals than in private situations.

When out in force at the Festival of Mind, Body and Spirit in London, the British Astrological and Psychic Society used to have a policy of allowing a Reader who couldn't link with a client, to pass him or her on to another Reader. Unfortunately, a number of folk used this to get extra readings for nothing. Nowadays, the Society only allows the client to change to another Reader if the reading blows out right at the start - not twenty minutes later. Time on a busy stand at a major festival is valuable and it can't be wasted on cadgers.

Off days

All Readers can have an occasional client for whom they can't seem to read, and this is especially prevalent for those who work on a clairvoyant or spiritual basis. All Readers have off days when they are ill, worried or just not in the mood for some reason or other. If you have such a day or even such a week, cancel your readings if you can, and reschedule them for another time.

Off lives

Even we have to admit that there are some Readers who simply shouldn't be doing this work at all. Some Readers become stale and bored with the job. Some are in it for the money and this shows only too well. Some are just not all that good. Such Readers aren't charlatans, they simply aren't really up to the job.

Disastrous Readers

There are a few truly ghastly male Readers who shouldn't be allowed to operate at all. These men view the women who consult them as potential sexual partners. Some even find themselves in court as a result of this. If you find yourself a victim of such a slime-ball, you may well wish to look for a good hit-man who will break a few of their bones! Bear in mind that hit-men are not spiritual and they charge more than Readers do, but nevertheless... More satisfaction will be gained by reporting the so-called Reader to your nearest association for that discipline, even if the Reader isn't a member.

And finally,

Sasha's stories...

For many years now, my main income has come from writing, and believe me it is even more difficult to make a living in this area than being a Reader. I still give the occasional Reading and I think it is entirely possible that I always will. My clients are neither friends nor acquaintances - they are members of the public: and while they may know me from my books and broadcasts, many of them have no idea that I am anything more than any other jobbing Reader. All my clients come on recommendation and, thank the gods, they all appear to be pleased and impressed with my services. Good. So what do I charge? I charge at least half as much again as the fees that we have recommended in this book, and my charges seem to go down well, whether the client has any idea of my fame or not.

The moral of this tale is that you can keep your integrity in this game, and furthermore, the more competent you become, the more value you can give, and the more you can justifiably charge for your skills.

CHARGES IN OTHER PARTS OF THE WORLD

It's all relative...

The scale of charges that Jan and I have suggested in this book, e.g. that of an equivalent price to a hairdo, a meal out or perhaps the hourly rate that a plumber or an osteopath would charge, should give you a clue wherever you are in the world, but you must take local conditions into consideration. For example, my suggestion of at least £40 per hour will amaze those who live and work in far flung parts of the UK, but it could disgust some American consultants. Just to give you an idea of the difference, here are a couple of snippets of information that we have gleaned from an excellent American magazine called The Mountain Astrologer.

A correspondent writing in to the letters page in the August/September 1998 issue complained that she had visited a Reader way back in the mid-1980s who gave her nothing more than a Sun sign reading, and that this consultant had charged her $180 for the privilege. My first thought was that the customer must have been a fool to go along for this reading without first getting a recommendation and also ascertaining the likely cost. In addition to this, we simply couldn't believe that any Reader would have the gall to charge that much a dozen or more years ago, and we wondered what Readers were charging now. In the December 1998 / January 1999 issue we found the answer. Marion March, who we know through her excellent astrology books, commented that in the mid 1970s when she started work, she charged $75 for a natal chart and $50 for a comparison. A more experienced astrologer called Barbara Watters told her to up her charges to $200. With a certain amount of trepidation Marion started to charge $200 for a personal reading and $300 for a written report - and her clientele grew rapidly! Her comment is that if you charge a high fee, the clients take their reading seriously, but if you charge a small fee they consider their visit to be nothing more than an amusing outing, and the astrologer's words are likely go in one ear and out the other.

It's all relative

We suggest that if you are in the outback of Australia, the wilds of Tunisia, the centre of a European city, the heart of California or the back roads of Tristan da Cunha, you look around and see what others who do similar kinds of work charge, and then set your prices accordingly. You will need to strike a balance between pricing yourself out of the market or giving away your skills for next to nothing, and somewhere around you there is a balance waiting to be found. Having said all that, I agree with Marion March that a higher price is always more successful than a lower one - probably for the reason that if your clients have to make an effort to find the money to consult you, they take the session seriously. Naturally, you must do your best to give a top-quality service to your clients, not to rush them too much, and to ensure that they get something really worth having for their hard-earned "dosh".

Jan doesn't give readings but I do. My first readings in 1973 were astrological ones and for those I charged £3. I now give an hour and a half to each client and although my preferred method of working is by astrology, I use palmistry if requested. I often tack a Tarot reading on the end of either a palm or a horoscope reading. My own charges are higher than those that I have suggested for an average Reader — but I am Sasha Fenton, and even if I don't always appreciate my own worth, my clients obviously do! However, compared to what I read in The Mountain Astrologer, if I went to the USA I would have to consider quadrupling my fees! Now where did I put that travel agency's phone number?

To summarise, charges should reflect the Reader's skill levels, modified to an extent by economic conditions in the area where you conduct your practice. An analogy to the medical or legal professions would not be far wrong; in those professions, you expect to pay a specialist far more than the general high street practitioner. The differing levels compensate the specialist or highly skilled person for the time, effort, training costs and running costs involved in reaching his level of abilities.

BUILDING A CLIENTELE

Advertising in local newspapers - word of mouth - business cards - other forms of advertising - ways of marketing your services - talks, lectures & demonstrations - the media - too many clients - nuisance phone callers - psychic fairs & festivals - school fetes or charity events

"If you have something you wish to sell, don't go whispering it down a well"
An American proverb.

If you have ever wondered what the difference between marketing and advertising is, you are about to find out. The first part of this chapter deals mainly with advertising and the second explores various forms of marketing.

Advertising in local newspapers

Advertising in your local newspaper is worth doing, but you will need to give this one a great deal of thought before jumping in. The problem is that dirty phone callers scan the personal columns looking for vulnerable women to call. If you are a male Reader, the problem won't be as great, but if you are female it might be worth wording the advert in such a way that it sounds as though you are man, or as though you have a male secretary. If you live alone or if you have a nervous disposition, you should avoid this kind of advertising. The whole point of advertising is to get your name and phone number around to the widest number of people, so the last thing you need to

The very best (and cheapest) form of advertising is word of mouth. If your clients are satisfied with your service and feel that it is good value for money, they will recommend you to their friends and colleagues. Clients that come on recommendation are already sold on your talents before they pick up the phone to make a booking. If you are just starting up, ignore our advice for a while about not talking about your work at parties and at the pub, and let the world know what you do. You will have to cope with a few "wise-asses" who make stupid or semi-nasty remarks, but some people will take you seriously and they will wish to consult you. Always carry your business cards with you wherever you go.

After each reading, give your client a couple of business cards and ask them to pass your name on to their friends. Also do the same with any literature that you produce.

Business cards

You don't need to spend a fortune on business cards. In the UK these days, there are machines in some shopping centres that print 50 white cards with black lettering for a very small amount of money. Such a machine may even be able to put a simple logo on your card - something like a lucky black cat or a sunshine face. If you are clever with computers, you can buy sheets that are specially designed to break into colourful card size pieces, and you can produce a few sheets at a time on your own home printer. Even proper printing is now far cheaper than it used to be, and there are mail order firms that will print business cards at a very reasonable rate with a choice of logo included.

You might wish to confine the information on your card to no more than your name, address and phone number as this will allow you to use the cards for other purposes in addition to your consultancy work. If you wish, you can simply put your divination and your phone number on your card - with or without a logo or fancy design. You can keep your cards simple or you can have something really fancy specially designed. The choice is endless and it is entirely yours. Take a look around your local high-street or shopping mall print-shop to see what can be done.

Sample business card:

JOHN DOE

Professional Astrologer, Tarot Reader, Palmist

12 Future Lane,   Tel: 0123 456 789
LONDON   Fax: 0123 456 789
ABC1 2DE   Mobile: 321 654 987
                                e-mail: leo@virgo.com

Never produce a large quantity of cards or literature at any one time. Printers will tell you that the unit price of each card is lower if you order them in bulk, but we can assure you that within three months of having a thousand of anything produced, you will change your phone number, your address, your name or your logo! Nice as it is to have really swish full-colour cards with your photo and a whole raft of dolphins, unicorns, Tarot cards and crystal balls printed on them, this isn't really worth the expense.

Leaflets are a cheap option and these can be done in colour and to any kind of standard, but be sure to use a bit of common sense here too. It isn't worth spending a fortune on colour printing or top quality brochures on expensive shiny paper, but on the other hand, crappy, down-market rubbish will give a very bad impression. Never run off large quantities of literature because you are sure to want to make changes to your information every few weeks. On the other hand, if you know you are due to work at a large festival where there will be thousands of people passing through, do ensure that you have plenty of everything on hand.

Other forms of advertising

A surprisingly cheap form of advertising is to put leaflets in shop windows or a card in an advertising rack in your local supermarket. You might pick up the occasional nuisance caller from this too, but perhaps not as many as you will through newspaper advertising. Avoid putting cards in cigarette shops or pubs, and stick to the supermarket where you should be more likely to attract women and other genuine clients. We have known Readers who placed cards in telephone boxes, but that strikes us as being extremely dodgy!

Here are a few ideas that you may wish to consider...

- Try your local gym or racquet club notice board.
- If you know any students, ask them to put a notice on their college board.
- Ask friends who work in large firms if they can put your leaflet on the notice board.
- If you specialise in horoscopes for children and babies, ask your local mother and baby shop to put a holder full of your leaflets out for you.
- Plastic leaflet stands and holders are extremely inexpensive and they will prevent your leaflets slipping down on to the ground and being trampled underfoot. It is a good idea to gum your business card onto any such holder to prevent the shop from using it for some other purpose.
- We have noticed some cafes hosting local news and adverts. There may be one in your area.
- If you work out of a local shop, employ a couple of youngsters to hand out your leaflets to shoppers. Do this on Saturdays or other busy times.
- You can slip leaflets into doorways and if your feet give out, you can pay local school children to do this for you. Always assuming that they do put the leaflets into the doors and they don't simply dump them and take your money for nothing.

Mail-order specialists will tell you that you can expect about a two to four per cent take-up on leaflets, so bear in mind that on this basis 200 leaflets will bring you four to eight clients. If you do try this route, keep your leaflets small and inexpensive. Each new client will pass the word (and your business cards) around to their friends and thus generate more business for you.

Ways of marketing your services

The following ideas will show you a variety of ways in which you can market yourself and your services. Some of them cost money, others actually bring in money, but they all take thought, preparation and effort.

Talks, lectures and demonstrations

Contact your local mother's group, wine appreciation society, garden club, Masonic Ladies, Rotarians and any other kind of group that uses speakers. You don't have to confine yourself to women's groups, but you are more likely to get spin-off business from women than from men, so consider the Townswomen's Guild, a mother and baby group, or anything else of the kind. You can locate such groups by asking around among your friends and colleagues and also by visiting your local library, because they may have a book in which members of the public note down any clubs or groups that they run.

Your local library may actually be happy to put on an event for you, or to add you to a series of local speakers and events that they are already running. Libraries take care of the advertising for this, but if you can drum up a few people yourself, this will help to swell the number in your audience.

You won't receive much money from any of these activities but they can be fun, you will meet nice people, and as long as you hand out your leaflets or business cards, you will get a few readings as a result.

If there are any self-development or self-awareness groups in your area, offer to give them a talk. If you are in the Spiritualist movement, you will be given opportunities to talk or to do readings for charity at Church or local centre events.

Charity organisations may be happy to use you, and sometimes even a local firm will book you as an after-dinner speaker. Some of these events will pay well, some will only pay your travel expenses, and some won't pay you at all, but they are all are worth doing.

Organisations like to book their speakers several months ahead, so ensure that you keep a diary and put everything down in it. Also keep any letters and other information in a file so that you can put your hands on it when you need it. You will definitely need to keep any contact phone numbers and a map or instructions of how to find the venue. Don't forget to take these with you when you set off for the venue!

Tips

If you are speaking to a group that isn't primarily into your subject, keep things very simple indeed. If you can give a live demonstration and/or involve your audience, so much the better. Sample Tarot readings, handing round crystals for people to hold, handing out pendulums or anything else of the kind, always go down well.

If you are talking to an "esoteric" group who are into your subject, ask the organisers about the standard of your audience and prepare your talk accordingly. If you happen to be dealing with a very high level audience, find out if the organiser can provide you with an overhead projector, and bring plenty of relevant material with you for the occasion. If you think you are likely to do more than the very occasional talk, treat yourself to a white board that you can take with you and a set of non-permanent markers.

If you are not used to writing business letters, make up something like the following example:-

---

A. Dowser
100 Main Road
Anytown
Yorkshire DD1 4QR
Tel: 0121 456-7890

1 January 2000

The Secretary,
The Wine and Garden Club
55 The Side Street
Anytown
County, State, Postcode (as appropriate)

Dear Sir or Madam,

If your club or society invites visiting speakers, you might like to consider me for one of your sessions.

I am a dowser and diviner who lives and works in your area, and I am available to give a talk to your club at a mutually convenient time during the next six months. I give a lively talk that explains what I do in simple terms. I like to bring along a selection of pendulums and dowsing rods, so that once I have demonstrated the methods, those members of the audience who would like to try dowsing for themselves can have a "hands-on" experience for themselves.

Should you be interested, kindly contact me at the above address.

Yours faithfully,
A. Dowser

> **Tip**
>
> If someone accidentally uses a permanent marker on your white board, you can remove the ink with acetone (nail-polish remover).

The media

There are ways of using the media to good effect. For example, if you can write (or if you have a literate friend who can ghostwrite for you), contact your local paper and see if they would like a feature on you. You could write a piece on what you do, how you got into the business and maybe even tell a couple of amusing stories about your experiences. You won't be paid for this, but if the paper prints your story, this will bring you to the attention of the public. Instruct the newspaper to pass your phone number on to anybody who enquires after a reading. If you need to take care about male callers, then ask them only to pass your number on to women.

Your local radio station may be persuaded to interview you, but they will probably want you to do some kind of reading on air. You may be asked to give a reading to the presenter of the programme, or directly to the public on a phone-in basis. If you can't cope with on the spot readings, then avoid broadcasting. If you are comfortable on the radio, you may be able to get a monthly spot in which you can suggest that people who want readings write in to you care of the radio station.

A small local radio station is a better bet for drumming up clientele than a nationwide network unless you specialise in phone readings. Make a point of getting the message across to the listeners that you are a professional Reader and that you don't give your services away for nothing. Even if you do make this clear, you will still receive letters from callers who expect you to phone them or write to them and to use your time and energy to put their lives right, at no expense to themselves.

One truly irritating form of free-loading is the person who writes (or worse, phones), asking you to teach them how to become a Tarot

Reader, etc. To their minds there is no reason why you shouldn't be happy to send them an eighty-page letter of instructions about how to read the Tarot, astrology or whatever. They will be more than happy for you to teach them the intricacies of your subject there and then over the phone! After all, how difficult can it be? It is easy to be seduced into a long session by a phone caller who has some knowledge but who wants to know "just one little thing," as this can easily drag you into giving the caller a five hour free tutorial there and then. If you have the patience to suggest schools and organisations who teach then do so, otherwise give the caller a vague answer like, "when you need a teacher, your Spiritual guide will be sure to send you one"; or, make it quite clear that you only work with proper appointments, like any other professional person.

Radio stations are besieged with Tarot Readers and so on who want to be on their shows, and producers and presenters are wary of newcomers or unknowns, so perhaps you should leave this until you have some kind of track record. If you really want the kind of credibility that will get you on the radio or the television, write a book and get it published. If you do decide to become a radio star, maybe work up some kind of divination that is a bit different from the norm, something like nine-star-key or Feng Shui for cats.

There are organisations such as the British Astrological and Psychic Society or the Faculty of Astrologers that issue Registers of Consultants, but you need to take one of their courses or become vetted by them before they will include you. The same applies in the USA, and the names and addresses of some organisations are listed at the back of this book.

Frankly anything you think up that gets your name around is worth considering, but the best advertising by miles and miles is the satisfied client who passes your cards on to others.

Too many clients?

After a while, you may become saturated with clients. We can almost hear you saying that you'd welcome that problem, or fat chance, or other words to that effect. Believe it, it can happen, and this also needs a bit of careful handling because it is tempting to try to see all those who call you. You will have to cope with the chagrin of putting off insistent callers and also of turning away all that lovely lolly, but in truth, you can't work yourself into the ground and you must avoid doing so. If you find yourself getting very busy, stick to a comfortable regime of work and don't add hours to those that you are already doing. If someone really wants to see you they will wait a few weeks, and if you can't fit them in at all, so be it. Maybe you have a friend or a colleague who can handle your overflow in the meantime, and then the client can come back to you at a later date. This does work well, and you may well get referrals from your friend at times when you are slack.

Take your holidays, take your breaks, get away from the job from time to time, enjoy your family, make love, make a cake, play with the kids. Take some time out to spend all the lovely dosh that you have earned and for goodness' sake, get a life!

Nuisance phone callers

As promised, we are returning to the subject of nuisance phone callers who target women. Even without advertising in the papers, you are bound attract a few dirty phone calls because this problem goes with the territory. The occasional nuisance call is easy enough to deal with. The caller wants a response, he wants to hear a woman's voice on the phone and to give himself a feeling of power. The worst of these awful men are those who phone in the middle of the night, because a call at three in the morning is always worrying, especially if you have elderly relatives or children who live at a distance from you.

If you have a man around, simply hand the phone over to him, because as soon as the caller hears a man's voice he is likely to put his own phone down. The caller doesn't want to deal with a woman who is "protected" by another male. If you don't have a man available, put the phone down and let the caller ring back and chat to your answering machine. If you have the kind of phone that is jacked into the wall, detach it for a half hour or for the night.

If you find yourself with a caller who is more persistent than the one-off nuisance caller, ask your local phone company for help as they (and the police) will be able to deal with it for you. The advent of new computerised phone systems now makes this option possible in a way that wasn't the case in the past. This is another good reason for having two phone lines - one for family and personal calls and a separate one for business. This way, if you receive a call in the middle of the night on your business line you can ignore it, and if you have to detach the phone for a while you will still be available to those who matter to you.

One horror story that we heard concerned a poor Reader who got a call from what appeared to be some kind of pay-phone that beeped continuously every time she answered the phone. The nuisance caller had rigged this phone to ring about a dozen times during the night and this problem went on for about eighteen months! The Reader tried to leave the caller to beep at the answering machine but after a couple of days, she discovered that he had found a way of rewinding the tape on her machine and listening to her messages. After a while, she put in a separate line for family and friends and fixed a removable phone jack onto the business line so that she could detach it at night. After about a month, the nuisance caller gave up.

Psychic fairs and festivals

We have already covered this to some extent in the chapter on places where you can work, and we will return to it in detail again in another chapter. It is still worth a mention here as a worthwhile form of marketing, especially if the festival is close to where you live.

The school fete or charity event

You may be happy to give readings for a few pennies at your school fete or charity event. Even if you hand over all your takings to the school or charity in question, this is a golden opportunity for you to hand out cards and literature.

Tip

Be very careful with any charity that is attached to a Church or other religious institution, as the people there may not like what you do. Some religious organisations are happy with palm reading or dowsing, but none of them want Tarot cards on their premises.

Sasha's stories...

Another Reader whom I shall call June, had a series of "heavy-breather" calls that rattled her badly. She had recently taken up with a new lover whom I will call Fred. Fred appeared to be very concerned and solicitous towards June about her problem. One day when June and I were discussing the calls, I had a sudden flash of psychic intelligence and I asked her if the calls ever came in when her boyfriend was around. June thought about this and then said, "Funny you should say that, but they always happen when Fred is at work."

My intuition told me that it was Fred himself who was making the calls - and it turned out in the end that I was right! Apparently Fred was doing this in a strange bid to make himself appear strong, protective and capable in June's eyes. Fred was obviously a nutcase and a few weeks later his behaviour towards June degenerated into such complete lunacy that she had to enlist the aid of her adult son and his friend to put him out of her house for good.

WRITING

Magazines – writing a stars column – phone lines – books – how to write a book – computers, disks & other nightmares – is it really worth writing a book?

I know before I even get my thoughts together on this issue that I could write a complete book on the subject — maybe one day I will!

Magazines

If somebody phones you and says that they are from some magazine or other, find out whether this is true or not! Many times the enquiry will be from a freelance writer who is hoping to sell an article to a magazine, and he or she will be happy to get you to write stuff that comes out under their name and to their financial benefit. Phone the magazine itself if you are in any doubt.

If the job looks "kosher", find out the following before agreeing to anything:

- Exactly what they want you to write about.
- How many words they want you to write.
- How they want the work submitted. They may want the work on disk in a particular word processing format (e.g. MS Word). They may want the work by Fax or by post.
- What the deadline is.
- How much they want to pay you.
- Whether they need illustrations from you and in what form.

- Whether you are the only contributor to the article or if you are one of a number of Readers writing on different divinations.
- Whether your name is going to be printed alongside your article, mentioned within it or left out altogether.
- Whether the article is likely to be edited to death or left more or less as you wrote it.

Always send an invoice with your work and then if this is not paid after 30 days, chase the invoice through the magazine's accounts department. You may have to send in a copy invoice, as quite often editors forget to send authors' invoices through to the accounts departments.

> *Tip*
> The copyright of your work should remain with you but it often doesn't - try to keep the copyright if you can; either way, never use exactly the same article in two different publications at about the same time.

> *Tip*
> Beware of writing anything for a Public Relations firm. These firms don't appear to value the time and effort, knowledge and skills that you put into your work. If my experience of several of these firms is anything to go by, you will have the devil's own job to get your fee out of them.

Writing a stars column

A stars column is great exposure for any astrologer, but it is hard work and you have to balance the time it will take against the income that this will bring. Jan and I have written many of these columns for daily, weekly, monthly, quarterly and annual stars. Sometimes the rate of pay has been laughable, and at other times it has been very good indeed. Some publications paid on the nail and others had to be chased to kingdom come and back. In one case Sasha was paid eighteen months after the job was done.

More than one firm got away without paying at all, because they knew that pursuing them through the courts would be more trouble and expense than we were willing to bear. One firm, which unfortunately, shall be nameless, wriggled out of paying almost all that they owed and then when we refused to work for them any more, they re-ran the previous year's daily and weekly stars columns, in the following year! Naturally, the firm kept every penny that this brought in and their activities almost ruined our reputation into the bargain, until we contacted the publications direct and stopped the columns that way. Legal action unfortunately tends to be more costly and time-consuming than it is worth - this is what these fraudsters count on.

Phone lines

If you are asked to record a phone line for a paper or a magazine, be very careful how you negotiate this. Find out exactly what the work will entail and what you will be paid for it. You should be safe enough if you are lucky enough to land a job for one of the large daily papers or a really reputable magazine. Unfortunately, this area is fraught with pitfalls and there are some phone line marketing firms who frankly aren't worth dealing with. It is very hard to work out what percentage of each minute of phone call time goes to which middleman and what proportion of a penny or of a cent is likely to come your way. Not all of these people are thieves, but too many of them are.

Whatever country you operate in, your best bet is to find another astrologer who knows the local scene and get as much of the lowdown on this tricky and complicated business as you can before agreeing to anything. Be very careful about any contracts that you are asked to sign (preferably have them vetted by a solicitor / attorney), and if you aren't given your copy of the contract properly signed by the phone company, stop work immediately, as this is a guarantee that they are not kosher.

Sasha's stories...

Many years ago, I asked the Commissioning Editor of the Aquarian Press what made him reject a book for publication, and he gave me the following four reasons:

- The publishers already had books of the same kind in print.
- The material sent in was so badly written or presented that it would need to be rewritten.
- The writer's idea was too specialised to appeal to a reasonably broad readership.
- The proffered manuscript had been channelled to the author by an alien in a flying saucer.

So now you know!

How to write a book

If you have a good idea, if you can write well and if you are lucky, you can be published. There are plenty of books around that tell you how to go about writing and how to prepare and present a book for a publisher, and you can find these books in your local library, but we will offer you a tip or two of our own. (The American Publishers' Marketing Association and Para Publishing websites are also valuable sources of information, useful in other countries as well).

Make yourself a very rough outline of the chapters and the content of your book but be prepared to deviate from this. Start the book by writing the meaty bit, that is the chapter that is the largest or the most important. Move to second most important section and gradually build the thing up until all you are left with are any oddments and fillers. Finally write the introduction. Leave this until last, because it is only when you have completed the book that you will know exactly what is in it and which are the points you want to emphasise most. Keep your introduction short because nobody wants to read a long one. Your introduction is your selling point as this is the bit that is read by the press, radio presenters and the public, even when nothing else is. Take a look at the introduction in this book to see what we are getting at.

Use a computer and regularly back up all your work on disks. Print off a "hard copy" of each chapter or of each day's work, so that you can see what you are saying on paper as well as on the screen. Be prepared to go back into chapters that you thought you had finished with, because you will come up with more ideas as you go along. Keep a running set of hardcopy (printed on paper), as an ultimate backup.

Don't worry about the speed of your typing, but do check your work through several times for spelling errors and other mistakes. We always reckon that a book goes through at least five drafts before we are satisfied with it, and Sasha is an old hand at this work. A beginner will fiddle about and alter bits and pieces over and over again until he is happy with it.

Treat yourself to a copy of The Writers and Artists Year Book (in the USA, buy The Writer's Market). From this, you can identify those publishers who produce the kind of book that you are writing. Send each publisher that you identify a synopsis of your book, some sample material from the book and some information about yourself. Don't forget to enclose a stamped addressed envelope if you want your stuff to be returned to you.

If after about six weeks, you hear nothing from a publisher, give them a ring. If your book is rejected, don't let this get you down. Please bear in mind that out of every half-dozen ideas that Sasha puts up to any publisher several times a year, one will be accepted. If Sasha were to cry over the ideas that have been rejected, she would never get around to drying her tears. Keep going, send the bloody thing out to another half-dozen publishers and see what transpires. If an editor rings you and suggests that he is interested in your work but that he wants something different from your original idea, see if you can adapt yourself to producing what he (or more likely she) requires.

Always use double spacing for your hardcopy, as this gives you and everyone else plenty of room for correcting and editing. If your software allows you to number the pages in each chapter, do so as this will save confusion if your pages happen to fall on the floor.

Sasha's stories...

Some years ago, to my absolute amazement, I read that it is bad form to send the same book outline to more than one publisher at a time. Apparently the proper form is to submit your stuff to one publisher and see if it is accepted, and only if the book is rejected to send it on to a second publisher, and so on. I recently read somewhere that multiple submissions (sending your idea out to several publishers simultaneously) are now becoming quite common but are still considered bad form. My answer to this is unprintable! The publishers may get fed up with the number of unsolicited outlines that they receive, but that is their hard luck. If you want to get a book accepted you can't be expected to wait for one publisher to look it over and send it back before sending it on to another - you will never live long enough. A number of UK publishers take months before responding to you. I once submitted an outline to a publisher who took a year and a half to respond, by which time the book had been published by someone else and it was happily sitting in the bookshops and selling well. You can imagine the relish in my voice when I told them this!

Computers, disks and other nightmares

The invention of the wordprocessor has been a boon to writers but it is now giving us some unexpected headaches. When Sasha wrote her early books, the publishers required two hard (paper) copies of a manuscript, whereas now they need a disk and one hard copy. In theory, whatever software you use should be easily converted to fit whatever the publisher uses. In fact, this is not always the case, and even when it is, strange errors can creep in. If you use an old steam-driven DOS program or something other than the mainstream type of software, it might not be convertible.

At the time of writing, if you use a PC or PC "clone" (that is anything that is not an Apple Mac), your best bet is probably to use Microsoft Word, although all the good word-processing programs are now largely compatible with each other. Even with computers that might be perfectly adapted for the modern world, bear in mind that books are always converted into a publishing or typesetting form that can cause odd things to happen to your text. You must read the page proofs through very carefully when they are sent through to you for checking. Now that Jan and I are publishing our own books we are seeing things from the other side, but our advice to writers hasn't changed.

Buy plenty of copies of your own book to hand around to friends and relatives. Be prepared to sell your books to clients and to those who attend any lectures that you give. You will be sent a few free copies of your book when your book is published, but after that you will have to buy further copies from your publisher. Your author's discount may be 30 per cent of the published price, 35 per cent or if you are lucky, 50 per cent. If your book has been around for a couple of years, ensure that you keep a good stock of copies on your own bookshelf in case it goes out of print.

The publishers should tell you when this is about to happen and you should then have an opportunity to buy up some or all of the "remainders", but sometimes this information doesn't get passed on and you can actually end up losing a copy of your own book for ever. If a book goes out of print, you can ask for the rights to revert to you, because you may one day decide to reproduce the book yourself. If you do this, you must have the text typeset again, because although the copyright for the text may be yours, the copyright for the typesetting and layout belongs to the publisher!

Is it really worth writing a book?

If you need to earn a living, book writing won't give you one. The best you will be able to earn is enough for a good annual holiday, but there are other spin-offs that far outweigh the money side of things, some of which are listed below:

- The moment that you get a book published, your credibility as a professional practitioner increases dramatically.
- You can put your ideas over to the general public and teach them the things that you want them to know.
- Writing a book is very satisfying, especially if it reaches the light of day.
- Even if the book goes out of print after a few years, you will still have a few copies of it around to show your grandchildren.
- A book is solid and real and it will still sit around on someone's bookshelf long after you are dead and gone.
- Nothing on earth boosts the ego like seeing your book in print - and why not? Writing a book and getting it published is a great achievement.

Chapter 16

MENTAL HEALTH AND WELL-BEING

Stress in the workplace – financial uncertainty – hours of work – living over the shop – the loneliness factor – dealing with too many peoples' problems – psychic self-defence – closing your chakras – more serious forms of self-defence – your own performance rating

Jan and I are the last people on earth to lecture people on health matters. We smoke, we sit for long hours at our computers and we sometimes forget to eat properly. However, there are a few sensible steps that we all can and should take, and even the two of us are beginning to wake up to the need for this. The first thing to bear in mind is that as a self-employed person, if you get ill you cannot work, and if you cannot work you won't earn any money, so you must try to look after your basic health in the best way that you can. You don't need us to tell you how to take care of yourself, because today's world is flooded with health information and you may have even more idea than we do ourselves. Having said this, there are a few traps that self-employed people fall into and even the two of us have to be aware of them and stay on top of them.

Stress in the workplace

There was an interesting article in our newspaper recently about stress in the workplace. The psychologists and doctors who had contributed to this item came to the conclusion that it was not the nature of a job itself or even the hours worked that caused the most stress, because the main problem is the negative emotions caused by working for difficult bosses. Feelings of powerlessness, rage, hopelessness, lack of appreciation, being treated disrespectfully and many more stresses of this kind can make any job of work a nightmare, while even a pretty awful job can be enjoyable if the employee is appreciated by a decent boss. Too many people dread having to go into work and they find it difficult to shake off their negative feelings even when they are away from the job. Self-employment solves this problem at a stroke, and as long as you enjoy the work that you do, you should live longer and feel better.

There are a number of problems attached to self-employment that you will need to consider. The following list will give you some idea of what they are, and as you read through this chapter you will see that we cover all of these points and more.

- The financial uncertainty of living with a fluctuating income.
- Long or irregular hours of work.
- Living over the shop and not really being able to get away from work.
- The loneliness factor or spending too much time at home.
- Dealing with too many people who have problems.
- Picking up psychic "crap".
- Not being able to judge your own performance rating.

Financial uncertainty
A number of the chapters in this book deal with financial matters and if you take the advice that is in them on board, you should be able to avoid some financial stresses. The following list sums up a few simple steps that you should consider taking.

- If you need a regular background income, do something other than to rely on your consultancy. Make this job as different from consultancy work as possible, so that it creates a kind of balance. Delivering milk, working in a factory, teaching yoga or using your brain in an academic way might be good part time alternatives.

- Always put away part of your income so that you have some savings behind you for a rainy day. (This issue is discussed further in another chapter).
- Keep good records so that your tax bill doesn't come as a nasty shock.
- Stay away from debts. Don't buy stuff you can't afford and don't need. Don't have accounts with every shop in town!
- Don't give away your savings to the first scrounger who asks for them. Remember that you have to be able to look after your own interests before you are in a position to help others.
- Spread the load by varying the kind of work you do. Therefore, give lectures, write articles, do some paid broadcasting or anything else that brings in a little money from a different source.

Hours of work

Try not to become so involved with your work that it becomes all consuming. If you begin to become successful your clients will pester you for appointments here, there and everywhere, but it is a poor policy to work too many hours. Clients will want to visit you when they fancy it and you can end up with appointments scattered throughout the week, tying up each day and preventing you from taking a really useful break. Work out a schedule of the kind of hours that suit your lifestyle and build in definite breaks in which you do something different. It is far more sensible for a dozen people each to make one minor adjustment to their schedules than for one person to try to accommodate a dozen people's individual circumstances. Think of your doctor, your shop on the corner - who sets their consultation or opening times, you or them? Don't just use your off days to catch up on housework or other chores, but designate true days off in which you visit friends and family, go on outings or simply laze around and take a rest.

Depending upon how much you need to work, you may have to see some clients in the evenings or at weekends. Don't fill up every weekend with appointments unless you really prefer to take your days off during the week. You may on occasion want to work throughout a day and an evening in one stretch, but as a general policy you would be better off either working during the morning and evening, or starting work in the afternoon and then continuing through to late evening. It will take time for you to establish a rhythm that suits you, but the main thing is not to allow the clients to bully you into seeing them on those days that you have selected for your free time.

If you are the type of person who needs a catnap in order to get through the day, then build in time for this and don't feel guilty about it. Every now and then, stop and count up the hours that you spend working, including any chores that are related to your business, such as doing your bookkeeping or buying equipment for your work.

If your consultancy has taken off and the hours that you are working are becoming ridiculous, consider raising your prices a little, as this will bring you in more money during fewer hours of work, and you may also find that you have a better type of client as a result. We all have limits to our physical endurance, and the concept of a weekend exists in order to take this into account.

Allow times during your working day for a break so that you can get something to eat and drink. If you want to take a walk around the block at these times, or sit and read a newspaper for half an hour, do so. In short, unless you are in dire financial straits, don't work yourself to death. Even then, don't do it for too long a period, however worried you may be; there's no point in all the hard work if you just end up with a heart attack or worse.

Patricia

This apparently irrelevant story is not actually about me, but about a Reader I once knew whom I shall call Patricia. You will see when you read through it, that it does have a point.

In the early 1980s the Fenton family fortunes were at an all-time low and my then husband, Tony, and I were working all the hours that we could to lift ourselves out of the mess. Up to this point, I had enjoyed being a Reader but I was beginning to feel pressurised by the amount of work that I was doing. In the words of a friend called

Eve Bingham who had been down the same road herself at various times in her life, I felt like a "reading machine".

In addition to working at home, I also worked on Saturdays at a psychic centre in London, and while there I became vaguely friendly with a Reader called Patricia.

Patricia seemed to have it all. She was tall, very slim, blond and pretty, and she had a magical air of confidence about her. She dressed in a slightly hippie style that suited her ethereal looks. Patricia was invariably happy. She was never lonely as she had a work partner called Jack, with whom she often shared stand space, and she seemed to have a happy and well-organised lifestyle. Patricia mentioned various "friends" who came and stayed with her some of the time. These friends were part-time boyfriends, and while the arrangement seemed a little odd, it apparently suited Patricia very well.

As I got to know Patricia better I discovered that she had four young children and no husband. Whether there ever had been one and what had happened to him is something that I never discovered. My admiration for this happy-go-lucky woman rose to monumental proportions. Inside my mind, Patricia was obviously a magnificently organised administrator, a wonderful Reader whose clientele stretched down the street and around the corner, a cook and a tireless homemaker par excellence, and much else.

During one conversation with Patricia I mentioned that the work I was doing was making me very tired. Patricia asked if I worked during the evenings and when I told her that I did, she suggested that I cut the evening work out. She said that she refused to work after dark as she found that the lack of daylight drained her psychic powers and made her tired. I said that many of my clients could not come to me during daytime as they had day jobs themselves. Her comment was that if they wanted to see me they would take the time off in order to do so. At that point in time I couldn't afford to turn away business, so I continued to work all hours. I simply took the point that Patricia must be so good that her clients wouldn't hesitate to find some way of getting to see her.

After a few months, I moved on from this venue, and it was several years later before I bumped into Patricia again. On this occasion I was shocked at her appearance. Patricia's complexion was pasty and her previously pretty face was bloated. She had put on a mountain of weight and she was clearly under a great deal of stress. She talked nonstop in a nervy kind of way and she couldn't stand still. Her nails were bitten down to the quick, her once long and lustrous blond locks were shorn and her hair looked lank and greasy. I asked her what on earth had happened to her. Patricia told me that her mother had died about a year earlier.

Apparently, during the "good" years, Patricia and her mother lived together in the house with the four children. It was her mother who had looked after the house and helped out with the children, and it was she who brought in extra money from various cleaning jobs. Patricia's mother obviously gave her ethereal daughter a whole world of love and support and she took the weight of reality off her shoulders. Patricia's various "friends" had been happy to contribute a little (or perhaps a lot) to her amazing and amusing household, and they were happy to revel in her beauty. Patricia had only needed to work a few hours a week in order to top up her income. Her work had been part hobby and part job and she could afford to be inspired by the spirituality of it.

Looking after a sick and dying mother and subsequently having to look after herself and her four children hadn't come into her game plan. Losing her looks, her "friends" and even her business partner all gave her a cold, hard dose of reality and she couldn't cope with it. I felt sorry for Patricia but it helped me to better understand my own role over the years. I realised that I had managed to work hard and bring up two sickly children with little help and that I had actually coped extremely well. However, I had tired myself out to the point of desperation during those difficult years, and as soon as I could reasonably cut down my hours of work, I did indeed take Patricia's good advice of not seeing clients after dark. I still don't, except on very rare occasions.

Living over the shop

This comes into the category of never getting away from the job, and all we can do is to repeat our advice to get out as often as you can, to take rest days and to take short holidays where possible. The suggestion that we made in a previous chapter of having a different phone for your work is also helpful, as you can simply leave this on the answering machine if you don't wish to be disturbed by client's enquiries.

The loneliness factor

If you spend too much time working from home, you can become extremely lonely. You may have clients roaming in and out day and night, but they are not friends and their contribution to your life is mainly financial.

You need to spend time away from home with your friends and family from time to time. It is a very good idea to include work at occasional psychic fairs in your schedule, because even if these are not always terribly lucrative, they give you an opportunity to get out of the house and to make friends and acquaintances amongst others who do the same work.

Networking can be useful for your career but it is even more useful as a break from working alone, or being with people who don't understand how it feels to do the work that we do. Some psychic festivals can be irritating but most are great fun, especially if you can get out afterwards for a meal or a drink with some of your new-found psychic friends.

Dealing with too many people with problems

The problem is the same for you as it is with therapists, psychiatrists and doctors, but intuitive work like ours is to our minds, even worse. Even those of you who don't work on a specifically psychic level, do pick up a lot of the misery or neuroticism that surrounds us during our working day, and this can cling to us if we are not careful, bringing us down. We can't always help our clients as much as we would like, so we can even feel guilty about our limitations. Just as a policeman can come to the conclusion after a few years that most people are crooks, we can come to the conclusion that most people are nuts, with our own nuttiness heading the list.

The answer, as always in this book, is to maintain a balance and to get away from the work scene from time to time. Having friends who also work in our field often helps, as they can share their experiences with you and this will help you to feel less alone or inadequate, and also to see the funny side of things.

Psychic self-defence

Techniques of psychic self-defence are useful in every walk of life, but in ours they are invaluable. A very apt comment came to us only the other day from a Reader called Rosa. Rosa said, "You give readings day in and day out and each person that comes to you does so because they have a problem or a dilemma in their lives. Every one of these clients leaves a little of their negativity behind them, and gradually this piles up on you until you yourself begin to be brought down by it." Wise words indeed, but what can be done about it?

The first thing that you should do is to clear your aura at the end of each working day. The method that we describe here was given to us by Eve Bingham.

Imagine clean clear water coming down from the universe, entering the top of your head and rushing through your body, and out through the extremities. Once you have done this, close down each one of your chakra centres and then do no more esoteric work for the rest of the day.

The chakra centres are spaced down your body and they can be imagined as a list of lights in the colours of the rainbow.

Here is a list of the chakras and their colours:

CHAKRA	POSITION	COLOUR
Crown	(top of head)	violet
Brow	(centre of forehead)	indigo/dark blue
Throat	(throat area)	turquoise blue
Heart	(centre of chest)	green
Solar plexus	(above navel, below chest)	yellow
Spleen	(lower/middle abdomen)	orange
Root or base	(base of spine)	red

How to close your chakras

Imagine that your body is filled with a bright white light that reaches miles up into the air until it is attached to the universe above you. This light also reaches down miles into the earth below you.

Turn off that section of the light that is beneath your feet.

Draw the light up your legs, leaving them in darkness.

Imagine a red glow at the base of your spine and then simply turn this red glowing light off.

Draw the darkness of night upwards through your body until the white light only reaches down as far as the middle of your abdomen.

Imagine an orange glow in the middle of your abdomen, then close this down.

Draw the darkness of night upwards once again, until your body is only lighted down as far as your diaphragm, and then imagine a glowing yellow light there. Turn the yellow light off.

Draw the darkness upwards from your diaphragm to the middle of your chest area and imagine a green glowing light there. Turn the green light off.

Draw the darkness upwards from your chest area to your throat where a turquoise blue glowing light is showing. Switch the turquoise light off.

Draw the darkness up to the centre of your forehead where you see a large dark blue eye. Close this eye down and ensure that it is completely shut.

Now take the remaining white light up to the crown of your head and move it away to a point just above your head and then imagine an amethyst water lily there (a lotus flower). Close this flower down tightly.

Send the remaining light up, up and away to the universe.

If you need to open your chakras before working or meditating or for any other spiritual purpose, you simply reverse this procedure.

It is also a good idea to take frequent showers and to wash your hair every day, as this will also help to keep the psychic and emotional "crap" out of your aura. It is very likely that those who work in our field are about the cleanest people on earth, because we shower and bathe so often!

More serious forms of self-defence

It is possible that you will be placed under some kind of psychic attack at some point in your life. This is not necessarily as serious as the kind of death threat that occurs in the Aboriginal pointing of the bone situation, or the "planting" of a Southern African Tokolosh doll that brings doom, gloom, death and disaster to all who have one sent to them. You may simply be among people who are jealous, spiteful, malicious, unkind and insensitive. Whatever the problem, as long as this is a relatively ordinary situation of the kind that gets everyone down from time to time, you can treat this by simply imagining yourself encased in a mirrored egg or a very shiny suit of armour. The bright shine will keep the unpleasantness and negativity away from you and it will reflect it right back to the perpetrators.

Once in a very blue moon, a Reader will find him or herself under a genuinely nasty psychic attack from people who know how to bring others down. The worst of all scenarios is where you are being blocked by some kind of malicious spirit, and this is very nasty because you can't get it out without help. Find a good clearance expert and have the damned thing exorcised! Even if this takes the whole gamut of bell, book, candle, holy water and a pricey fee, it will be worth it. If you are in the south east of England, you could try contacting Molly-Ann Fairley who is listed in the appendix at the back of this book. Molly-Ann uses a simple yet powerful healing technique that is very successful in such cases.

If you think that your place of business is being bugged (or buggered) by a spiritual force, a quick method of clearing this is to open your chakras and then imagine the malignant spirit being taken away up into the light. After you have done this, use your imagination to fill the space up with clean, clear, pale blue water, from the ground up to the roof. This will stop the malignant force from returning.

Finally, ask your god or gods to bless the location, and for it to be a peaceful and prosperous place for you to work in. If the situation continues and/or if there are any poltergeist or other psychic phenomena going on that you are not happy about, call in a team of exorcising mediums to clear it.

At this point in our ruminations, the two of us are tempted to ask ourselves how many other business books advise people to clear themselves or their place of work of spiritual mischief, or better yet to call in an exorcist! Jan spent 31 years in banking and he still raises an eyebrow at the very thought of psychic clearances and so forth, but he has seen and experienced enough of the spiritual world over the years to understand what can happen.

The foregoing ideas might appear potty to some of you, but they are not quite so daft when you consider that people in Oriental countries call in Feng Shui experts before planning the construction of a building and opening up for business, especially in banking and other large corporate businesses. Why not buy a book on Feng Shui and use it to improve the layout of your business premises?

Your own performance rating.
"What if all the other Readers are better than I am?"

We are all occasionally assailed by feelings of doubt or the certainty that other Readers are better than we are ourselves, and such feelings can sap our confidence. The best approach is to look at the results of your own work and to consider whether your clients are happy with what you are doing for them. If your clients are happy, that is all that matters, so just be yourself and get on with the job in your own way. The following comments may help you to put this problem in to perspective.

Unless you actually see your fellow Readers at work, all you have to go on is what they tell you, and human nature is such that they will inevitably boast about their successes. If a Reader does tell you about a failed reading, then this is likely to be put down to the fact that, "the client was in denial and refused to accept anything that was said to him," or some other such excuse. Also bear in mind that Readers vary a great deal in their approach, and clients also vary a great deal. The chances are that a more forthright and confident Reader who thinks he or she knows it all, or who likes to hector a client "for his or her own good", won't necessarily please a sensitive or nervy client half as much as a more diffident, careful type of Reader would.

Even if you see other Readers at work and find them impressive, remember that you can't see yourself at work, which makes it impossible for you to judge your own performance. Also bear in mind that we all have good and bad days and you may be seeing someone at a time when their "form" is at its best. They may not be half as good the rest of the time.

Keep a note of your achievements over the years; they are easy to forget, but if you have a record of them you can read it and bring back your sense of perspective. In fact, compile them into a Curriculum Vitae (CV), because you'll need one occasionally, and you'll certainly need a Bio sheet (promotional material to hand out to radio interviewers, newspapers, etc.).

Sasha's stories...

After all my years in this business, I'm still basically a shy person, and sometimes I tend to have less than total confidence in myself. When I am faced with the outgoing and dogmatic type of Reader who tells me how good he/she is, or who puts on a wonderful performance, I very quickly find myself thinking about my own approach. Well, in 25 years, I have never been short of clients when I need them, and people out there have bought over five million of my books, so I can't be doing much wrong, can I?

Similarly, as you achieve various milestones in your Reading career, keep them in mind, they will help you to keep your perspective and self-confidence in your abilities.

ORGANISATIONAL METHODS

Your appointments – the telephone – secretarial skills – letterheads – files & filing – time management – travel & transport

Now we are going to look more closely into the business side of the business, and for this you will look into the basic business skills that you will need.

The other day, we were watching a television programme about the paranormal. We were interested to note that one of the mediums who travelled out to his clients and to give talks and demonstrations, left all the arrangements relating to his business to his brother. Clearly the brother had a good grasp of organisational methods and he was comfortable using a computer to keep track of the medium's appointments and financial arrangements.

In our own case, Jan and I are both extremely capable administrators, but to save time and energy, we split these duties between us, often acting as each other's secretary or bookkeeper. The chances are that when you are just starting out on your new career, you will have to do these things alone, just as I did before Jan came into my life. Whether you look after your own business or whether you have help, this chapter will give you the information that you need to make a success of the admin side of your business.

Your appointments

Just like any other business person, you *will* need a diary. You can use a Filofax type of arrangement, a pocket computer or a desk diary, just as long as you can find the information when you need it.

Scribble anything and everything down in this diary and even when the year ends, keep your old diary because you may suddenly need to look back to find a name, a phone number or an address. If you jot down a client's phone number against her name when she makes the appointment, then you have it handy if you need to change the date of the appointment for some reason.

We use a large index book in which to record important names, addresses and phone numbers. Jan has always used a computer organiser, and he runs off a printout of these from time to time. This also helps us when we want to produce a mailing list, as the organiser can easily print out labels on envelopes; it also means that we have fewer incorrectly addressed envelopes, as the computer is much more accurate than using handwritten addresses, besides looking far more professional. Both systems work well. Clients' names and numbers don't always need a permanent record, but if they are scrawled down somewhere in your desk diary, you can locate them again if you need to.

The telephone

This is one of the best inventions of the 20th century (in our opinion, it ranks alongside the washing machine as a mark of true human progress!). The telephone can also be a tyrant. In the days before the invention of answering machines, Readers had to take calls day and night, whether they wanted to or not. One could leave the phone off the hook in those days, but if you try that now, the phone will soon start to squeal at you! You will definitely need an answering machine, but these are no longer expensive. The best kind of machine is one where you can listen into an incoming call if you wish, but where you can turn the sound down or off if you don't.

There is nothing more irritating both to yourself and your client than to be interrupted by incoming calls. If you happen to be in a spate of receiving many enquiries, it might be better to keep your phone and your machine away from your workroom. A ringing or clacking machine will disturb both you and your client during your reading. If your client hears you dealing with too many other callers, he or she can get the erroneous idea that you are making a fortune, and he will certainly feel that he isn't getting the attention he deserves in his reading. Obviously, you need to monitor your machine in between clients and to catch up with your calls.

If friends call while you are working, tell them you're busy and will call them back later. If your family are happy to answer calls for you, fair enough, but this is an imposition on them, and it might even be worth considering having a mobile/cellphone or a second land line for your work.

Even as we put this book together, the phone companies are improving their services all the time, so do keep up with the latest trends, as you will probably find a use for these, as and when they come on to the market. Call waiting, voice-mail and / or an answering service might be useful to you. Our guess is that the e-mail will also prove very useful to those of you who have a home computer.

Secretarial skills

If you give lessons or lectures, or if you have to write letters or send invoices, you will need something to type on. If you can't type, you might consider taking a course of lessons for keyboarding, and perhaps also for general secretarial skills. You don't need to type particularly quickly or accurately these days, because computers are so much more user friendly than typewriters. You will need some basic business knowledge in order to make up a business letter or to put your training material down on paper.

Nowadays it can be as cheap to buy a computer as a typewriter once was, and if you decide to run to something like this, you will never regret it. If you are an astrologer, you will definitely be into computing as a normal part of your job.

Letterheads

The last thing you need is to buy a heap of expensively printed letterheads for your business. If you can use a computer or if you have a friend who can, then make up something suitable and keep a couple of dozen sheets handy. If you can set up some kind of letterhead on your computer, so much the better, as this will print itself out at the top of every letter that you write. You can use coloured letters in any number of colours or fonts these days. A font is a name for the style of letters you choose to use, e.g. President or Cooper Black, or Times New Roman.

Sample letter:

A. Reader
22 Main Street
Anytown
(County / State / Province)
Postcode xxx xxx

21 May 1999

The Secretary
The Astrology and Psychic Group
414 Long Lane
Newtown
(County / State / Province)
Postcode xxx xxx

Dear Secretary,

Thank you for your invitation to come and talk to your astrology group on the 5th of May 2000 at 7 pm. at the small hall in Newtown. I am pleased to be able to tell you that I will be able to attend. Could you please let me know whether you have a white board or an overhead projector available, so that I can organise the materials for my talk accordingly. Also, could you please send me a map showing the exact location of the venue and the parking arrangements.

Yours sincerely,

A. Reader

Sample invoice:

A. Reader
22 Main Street
Anytown
(County / State / Province)
Postcode xxx xxx
(Country)
10th May 1999

Invoice No: 18
For giving a talk to the Astrology and Psychic group at the small hall in Newtown on the 5th of May 1999.

Total invoice: £50 ($75)

Keep a record of your invoice numbers, they should run consecutively, and the numbers are useful if you have to chase up payment. (This is often necessary).

Keep a copy of every invoice you send out. You must have them available so that you can keep track of money owing to you, details of the money you've made during the tax year, and also for the possibility of the details being required for a tax office query.

You should go through your invoices at least monthly, and chase up outstanding amounts. This is a necessary evil, there are always some slow payers, and you have to chivvy them up. You can not afford to have useful money sitting in other peoples' pockets when it rightfully belongs to you.

Here are three really great timesaving tips.
- Have an admin blitz every couple of days. Open your post, deal with paperwork and bills, file things and get them out of the way. If you pile stuff into a tray and leave it, you will only have to plough through it again later, and you will lose track of important bits of paper.
- Elect special days and times for seeing clients and stick to them. Elect days for family stuff, housework, working on the car, visiting your lover and so on - and stick to them.
- Make batch bookings for your clients so that you don't break up the flow of your day. (More about this in a minute.)

Files and filing

We all have a few old cardboard shoe boxes lying around, and a couple of drawers into which one can shove stuff with the idea that "when I have time, I'll sort those papers out properly...", but we can tell you categorically that this sorting never happens!

If you're running any sort of business, there is only one thing to do: get a few large files *now!* Label them (in pencil, then you can easily change the labels) correspondence, and whatever other headings you wish for the types of paper filing you accumulate. You'll need to keep letters to refer to, and any number of other things that are useful, including your receipts, accounts, notes, etc.

If you have a tray for the filing, then you can do it every couple of days, and you'll find that once you're in the habit of it, it's actually quite fun to file your documentation away. It's definitely a great help and most of your papers can be filed in date order, but the main thing is that they will be far more accessible than scratching through your bottom drawer - especially after your children have dumped the drawer out to make space for their toys/comics/other invaluable kiddie purposes. Keep copies of all letters that you write and send out.

Keep all incoming letters. Tear out interesting articles from magazines that relate to your divination - that saves space instead of keeping the whole magazine if there's little else that is of interest in it. But do get the files and use them, you won't regret it.

Time management

The third item in this list of tips is worth a little thought. Your clients are unlikely to fit their visit to you into a tight schedule, because however busy their lives are, they will invariably take the day or the evening off so that they can relax, enjoy their reading and mull over it afterwards. A client's visit to a Consultant is an occasion and they are happy to drag it out as long as possible. For many clients this is probably the only time in their lives that someone else concentrates exclusively on them. Inexperienced Readers often find that a client has taken up a whole afternoon or evening, and while the Reader has probably enjoyed helping his client, he invariably wakes up to the fact that as far as the reading was concerned, his hourly rate of pay worked out to less than that of a toilet attendant in a third-world bathhouse.

You can avoid this problem by booking several clients in at suitable intervals during your allocated work sessions. Work out how long each reading should take and add 15 minutes to each allotted appointment. (Astrologers and palmists usually need more time, because they need to prepare palm prints or chart printouts). This means that the most time that a client can run over is 15 minutes, because he or she will be aware of the next client arriving, which will trigger the fact that the appointment is at its end. If you do only have one reading booked in for the day, or if your last client looks set for the duration, there are ways of dealing with this, too.

In the chapter where we discuss equipment for your workroom, we mentioned that you can use a candle as a timing device. We aren't advocating the ancient method of cutting notches in a candle and using it as a clock, but something much simpler. The following idea was given to us by Lindsey, the hairdresser/astrologer from Southend. She told us that she always had a lighted candle on the go while she did her readings. When she felt that the appointment should come to an end, she stood up and snuffed out the candle, and she didn't sit down again. Lindsey said that these activities had the psychological effect of transmitting the fact that the reading was finished without her having to actually say so. Of course, there is always the straightforward approach, i.e. by pointing out politely that the allocated time is nearly up, enough time for a last question, etc., but some people prefer their individual ways of closing of the session.

Travel and transport

Unless you are going out to give a talk or for a party-plan session, only visit clients in their own home if you know them well, if you really want to or if you have a great urge to be a social worker. The time and money you spend on travelling, finding the infernal place and parking are only part of the problem. If someone asks you for a house call, it is probably because they are elderly or infirm and while there is no reason why these people shouldn't have access to your services, what they really want is company. These lovely people will ply you with tea, home-made cakes and show you photographs of their grandchildren, and while this is all very well, is it practical it on a business basis? You may read this and still wish to do it, and that is fair enough. Too much of this, however, is guaranteed to ensure that your costs - in time and physical exhaustion as well as money - will far exceed your income. You can't make losses like this for very long.

We are also a little wary of suggesting that you go unaccompanied into a stranger's home, as you can't always be sure of your safety.

Sasha's stories...

Having said this, even such a potentially foolhardy activity can have an educational value. I remember once, years ago, visiting a client who said that she had no way of coming to see me. This client was a gentle, slim, beautiful young woman whose clothes were far more fashionable and expensive than anything I could have afforded. She appeared to spend her days sitting in a very nice apartment and doing nothing other than watching the television.

Her reading revealed a life that was strangely empty but extremely comfortable. Once I had gone through the main points of what I could find on her Tarot cards, her conversation turned very strange. She seemed to be quietly and gently crazy. She went on about how tigers came through the walls at her, and much else of the same ilk.

It transpired that she lived with some rock star or other, and that her fragile mental state had not been helped by the liberal doses of illegal drugs that she was pumping into herself. For a moment I envied her, as my own life has always been one of hard work and the complete opposite of her existence as a beautiful, pampered "lily of the field".

But, after a bit of thought, I knew that nothing would induce me to exchange my lifestyle for hers - anyway, I couldn't have afforded all those drugs!

LEGAL AND OFFICIAL MATTERS

Tax – legal problems

While researching this book we talked to a number of Readers, all of whom had something of interest to tell us, much of which is now scattered around the various chapters of this book. However, there are two stories from among the many that we heard that deserve special treatment, and we have created this small chapter to accommodate them.

Tax

Our astrologer friend, Sue Lilly, told us of a case of a therapist who was recently investigated in minute detail by the tax department. The tax inspector looked over this guy's books right back over a period of six years, and he also asked to see the therapist's diaries for those years so that he could match the number of appointments to the money that this man had paid into his business account in the bank.

Having spoken to a number of taxation and VAT people ourselves over the years, we are of the opinion that tax people must have had some kind of suspicion about this therapist. As it happens, no tax anomalies were found and the therapist now has a clean bill of taxation health. Other Readers in our field suggest that the tax people do tend to be suspicious about us because we handle so much cash and they may feel that we must be earning much more than we are declaring.

Our experience of the tax inspection department's people is that, when they see the reality of a typical British Reader's earnings, they wonder how we manage to live! The answer here is, as always, to keep receipts and to declare your earnings, and then either get help from the tax office with the self-assessment forms or to use a good accountant.

Legal problems

You will have noticed how in the introduction to this book we have used a disclaimer. We have explained that this is mainly for the litigious American market because malicious or frivolous legal cases are a rarity in Britain. However, we have just recently heard of a very disturbing case which we will investigate further while putting the finishing touches to this book.

We are aware that even in Britain there are a few clients who will ask a Solicitor (in other countries, a solicitor is known as an Advocate or an Attorney) to sue a Reader for an unsatisfactory reading.

Our advice has always been that in Britain, a reading is deemed to be a matter of a verbal contract between a Reader and his client. If the client decides to have this service performed for him and especially if he then pays for this service, he has accepted the contract for what it is worth, on face value. If he then decides that he doesn't much like the "goods", that is the client's hard luck. In the one or two cases that we have heard of where a client has tried to take his case to a Solicitor, the upshot has been that the case (and the client) were thrown out.

It is up to all of us who give readings to consider the idea of buying the kind of indemnity insurance that doctors have, and also of printing a disclaimer of some kind on the backs of our business cards.

Naturally, the situation differs from country to country, and the best thing to do is to be a member of an organisation for your specific discipline, as these will normally be up to date on such issues, and sometimes may also be in a position to help their members in difficulty. None of us claim to be all knowing, we only see shadows of the future, and fortunately the vast majority of clients understand this.

Adam Fronteras, chairman of BAPS, tells us that Readers can be sued for giving specific financial advice. He says that if a Reader tells a client to sell his house at a certain date in order to make a profit, and if this does not work out profitably for the client, he may have grounds to sue the Reader. The same principle is very likely involved regarding specific medical advice, and these two points certainly apply in the USA as well as the UK. We suggest that you read the wording of our disclaimer (at the front of this book) again, carefully. In short, a Reader is not legally qualified to give specific financial or medical advice.

As is often the case, problems usually only arise when there is a prior misunderstanding of what our services actually comprise.

Chapter 19

AN OVERVIEW OF FINANCIAL MANAGEMENT

To be legitimate or not – when to open a bank account – what kind of bank account – the benefit system – budgeting – savings schemes – make a will

> "Annual income twenty pounds, annual expenditure nineteen and six, result happiness.
> Annual income twenty pounds, annual expenditure twenty pounds ought and six, result misery."
> *(Mr. Micawber's advice in "David Copperfield" (published in 1850), by Charles Dickens.)*

Jan comments that the above advice is still completely valid, and that half of our problems simply relate to fully identifying what our expenditure is; most of us have no problem in identifying what our income is!

The world of a Reader is not unlike that of an artist or actor, and such creative folk aren't always keen on the business side of things, but we *are* in business and it is better to acknowledge that fact and to take control of the situation. The first thing to consider is your lifestyle, and it would be worth looking at the following list of questions and answering them as though they were part of a quiz. If your lifestyle changes in the future, you can always reread this section and see what adjustments you need to make.

Do you have a full or part-time job in addition to your consultancy?

Are you retired or living on a pension?

Are you home-based and receiving housekeeping money from a partner?

Are you a full-time consultant with no other form of income?

Are you disabled? Can you work in addition to receiving disablement benefits?

What level of income do you need from your consultancy?

To be legitimate or not to be legitimate

If you are only doing the occasional reading for people who you know personally, the payments that you receive will be in cash and they are of no real importance, but you must be aware that even this level of undeclared money-earning is actually illegal! The moment you become truly professional or you are dealing with the general public, you must put the whole thing on a professional footing for your own safety's sake.

Sasha's stories...

During my time as a full-time professional Reader, about three times a year an envelope from the Department of Social Security would plop through my letter box. This would contain a form asking for my National Insurance Number (Social Security Number) and for details about my earnings.

Since giving up reading for a living, I have never once received one of these enquiries, thus confirming my conclusion that once in a while one of my clients would either deliberately or inadvertently mention my work to the Department of Social Security. I have no idea who it was who "shopped" me on any of these occasions, or what their motives for doing so might have been.

Fortunately for me, my work was always legitimate, so when these forms arrived, I happily filled in my National Insurance number and give the DSS the name and address of my accountant. My accountant never said whether he had been contacted by any of these officials or not, so I presume that he wasn't.

When to open a bank account

You should open a separate bank account for your business as soon as any of the money you earn goes beyond the level of an occasional bit of pocket money. You need to see clearly what is and what isn't part of your consultancy's income. If you have another full or part-time job, or if your partner gives you housekeeping money, you need to know whether you can budget on this with or without your Consultancy income. If your Readings are your main source of income, you need to know exactly what is coming in from them and what is being spent. The second reason for a separate account is for tax purposes, so that you can see what profit you are making and then work out (or ask your accountant to work out) what your tax liability will be. Anybody who is in business for themselves needs to save a percentage of their income throughout the year for tax purposes, and unless this money is clearly separate from all your other income, you won't know what you should be putting by.

What kind of bank account should you look for?

Shop around, because banks offer many different kinds of costs and services, and as they become increasingly competitive in the future, they will offer even more. Some banks offer a free £50 overdraft and current accounts that pay interest, but this may only apply to a personal account and not a business one.

You may wish to open a deposit (savings) account in addition to a personal current one, so that you can shovel aside the money you will need for tax and other matters.

Banks the world over give out literature on their services, so pick all of this up, take it home and compare the services that each bank offers. If you already have a bank account, you may wish to stay with the same bank because it is easier to move money from one account to another when needed.

These days, you can move money around by phone or even via your computer, as long as the accounts both belong to you, thus saving you from having physically to visit your bank and wait around in queues.

You may wish to have accounts at different kinds of financial institutions. Just get all the literature or make an appointment for a chat with the business banker at your branch, and see which scheme will best suit you.

The benefit system

Depending upon the country you live in and your own personal circumstances, you may be in receipt of some kind of benefit. This benefit might be an old-age or disablement pension or a form of family credit or income support. The rules and regulations of what you can and cannot earn differ in each case, and you will need to look into these to see what your particular position is. There will be a level of income or a number of working hours that you should not exceed, or it may not be tax efficient for you to earn over a certain amount.

It is impractical to give specific advice on this subject in this book, but we suggest that you do a complete survey of your position and then make the most effective decision that you can.

Budgeting

Whatever your lifestyle, it is worth working out a weekly or monthly budget so that you know what you actually need to live on. After Jan's 31 years in banking and my 25 years in self-employment, we can tell you that we both loathe doing this, as the fact is that we often need more money than we actually have! Perhaps when our publishing business really hits pay-dirt, we will become so rich that we won't have to think about budgeting, but our belief is that plump pink pigs will fly past our office window before that day comes.

If like us, you are not amongst the mega-wealthy, you must grasp the nettle and work out exactly what your expenses are and what you really need to have coming in. Read our comments in the chapter on Cashflow.

Remember to bear in mind that you will also need to keep some money by for the tax-man and a number of other purposes.

Savings schemes

If you are earning enough to live on and have something left over, get into the habit of putting ten per cent of your income away for the future. The way you do this is immaterial. You may start out with a china piggy bank and then graduate to some other kind of savings scheme.

If you are the type of person who can't keep your hands off the piggy bank, then find a scheme that allows you to save on a monthly basis.

In the UK, you can save with a bank, a building society, in private schemes of many kinds and with the Post Office. Bear in mind that if you use a broker or a financial advisor, a percentage of your money will go to pay his or her commission, so try to keep things simple and use something ordinary. Having said this, once you have a substantial amount of money available for investing, sound financial planning advice becomes more important; get professional advice, even if only on an infrequent basis.

You may wish to investigate the "direct" schemes that allow you to deal directly with the various investment companies without handing over commission to a middle man. If your finances are complicated, an accountant or a financial advisor might be a necessity and any fees or commission that you pay out could be worthwhile. You may wish to look into an ISA or a savings bond, or whatever investment schemes are available in the country where you live.

In the USA and elsewhere, there will be many financial organisations happy to help you save. Once you have accumulated a fairly large sum, say for example, the equivalent of £500 or perhaps $1,000, you may wish to put such amounts away in a medium-term scheme such as a bond, or an equity scheme that invests in the stock exchange.

Pension schemes vary tremendously and some are better than others, so this too is an area where advice is needed. If you are middle-aged, it may not be worth taking out such a pension plan, whereas if you already have one, it may be worth topping it up. Advice will be needed here.

The above comments are basic "Sasha advice", but I now hand you over to my ex-banker husband, Jan for his views...

OK, here we go. As we've pointed out in our disclaimer at the beginning of the book, we are not trying to supplant professional financial advice. We provide you with views and information that may be useful in your overall planning, and the best way to present this to you is along the lines of the following "golden rules" that both of us have developed for ourselves.

- Right from the start, put ten percent of your income aside as savings. If you don't think you can afford to do this, think of how much worse off you would be if you *don't do it*. How will you get that new computer, or replace your car when it coughs and splutters to a grinding halt?
- Put your ten percent away as you get paid, not after you've first done all your shopping. Use a system that suits you - put the money into a piggy bank, under the bread bin or wherever, but put it away somewhere *separate* from the rest of your money. If you deposit your earnings into a bank account frequently then use that opportunity to split your deposits accordingly.
- Don't touch your savings until you've accumulated enough to cover all your regular expenses for a six month period. Having done that, still don't touch the money except to transfer it somewhere less accessible! Put it into a 30 day deposit account for example, but not into any long term investment that won't let you access it fairly swiftly in an emergency.
- Then, continue saving, but this time you can put some goals into place. Make a list of what you will want to save for - a new computer; that holiday you've been promising yourself; another car, etc. (You should be saving in addition to the usual things like life assurance, pension plans and so on; the ten percent won't be enough to include these as well. Keep your insurance premiums, etc. in mind when calculating your six months' worth of expenses as mentioned above).

- Scout around for investment accounts, in the bank, Post Office, or elsewhere that will pay interest (preferably on daily balance) monthly. If you are paid interest annually or even six-monthly, you are losing the opportunity to earn interest on interest, which is a very useful multiplier for the growth and health of your savings.
- Reinvest the interest earned on your savings, don't withdraw it. If you do, then in fact your savings don't stay the same, they lose value due to inflation. £100 or $100 is worth quite a bit less in five years time than it is today
- When you have accumulated a substantial amount of savings - say, a few thousand pounds or dollars, then think about (a) not having all your eggs in one basket, (b) improving the return on your investments, (c) splitting your savings into portions for short, medium and long term goals. Get some professional advice at this stage.
- Be careful about investing in the stock exchange unless you happen to be just about a professional at it yourself. You can't do this well just by reading the newspapers - by the time news and tips come out in the papers, it's already too late for you to do much about it. Unit trusts and similar investments are a different story, because these are managed daily by the ex-

Jan's stories...

If you have a mortgage bond, you may have the potential for a very useful form of savings. By putting money into your bond, the effect is that you are getting a return on your money equal to the mortgage interest rate *after tax*. The question is, whether or not you are allowed by the institution to withdraw that money again when you want to. In South Africa, I was fortunate enough to be working for a progressive bank (Nedbank), that not only adopted this system, but was the first bank there to expand the option to include vehicle leases. You can now even withdraw the extra money you put in, by using your bank card in an

ATM (or cash card machine, as they are called in the States). I was surprised to find a couple of years ago that no UK banks had any such schemes available. I came across a variety of excuses why this was an impossibility, but none plausible enough to counter the fact that one would expect a first world country to be able to outdo little South Africa! Having been closely involved in the Nedbank developments, I surmise that the hold-up in the UK was probably due to a mixture of (a) legislative restrictions, (b) concern about a loss of profits and (c) the inability of the banks' computer systems to administer such a concept. However, I know that in South Africa, we surmounted all these obstacles and more, and I'm pleased to see that at least one institution here (Virgin / Bank One) has now introduced a very similar type of system. This means that others will have to follow if they want to stay competitive, so keep your eyes open...

perts for you. Even then, their value can fluctuate quite a bit, so don't put all your savings into these investments.

Finally... make a will

Make a will. You don't need to think about your own mortality, but you do need to ensure that what you leave will go where you want it to - even if this is only to the local donkey sanctuary. You can buy forms and do this for yourself, or you can use a solicitor.

If you marry, divorce, remarry or in any other way change your circumstances, you will need to make a new will as any previous one will usually become invalid. Check out the situation in your country.

Chapter 20

CASHFLOW

Budgeting – Fluctuations in the flow of clients – times of optimism & pessimism – psychic self–defence

For those of you who are not familiar with the language of finance and business, the word cashflow relates to the amount of money "flowing" into, and out of, a business over a period of time.

It means having enough money behind you to carry you through those times when money is slow to come in. In a normal business situation, a cashflow problem may arise when a manufacturer has bought the raw materials for a job of work, done the job and is now awaiting payment.

The same situation may arise when a small shopkeeper stocks his shop and then waits for the customers to come along and buy the stock. If the manufacturer and shopkeeper have surplus funds in the bank, this period of waiting is easy to ride out, but if they don't have such funds, they find themselves in various levels of trouble.

As a Reader you shouldn't have cashflow problems of the stock-holding kind, because what you are selling is a service rather than actual goods, and the only stock in trade that you carry are your skill and knowledge. The only possible stock item might be the ream of paper that an astrologer buys which he needs for printing his charts or reports out on.

Your problem comes when the supply of clients suddenly dries up. You need to pay your rent or your mortgage, you still have to eat and you may also be making payments for a car, a computer or some other item of equipment, all of which becomes difficult when business ceases to flow through your door.

Budgeting

Doing up a budget will help you to take control of your finances, instead of them running your life for you. If you don't control your money situation, it will mess up your business for you. If you get on top of it, you'll get your beauty sleep at night and you'll make your future secure. And, if you keep things simple and take one step at a time, it's not difficult.

In doing up your budget, you want to include all your likely income items, and - even more importantly - all your likely expenses. Include even little things like the daily newspaper. If this costs you 75p or $1, then in a year you'll spend just over £200 ($260) on the papers. And that's excluding the weekend papers. Throw in another half dozen similar small items and you're talking in terms of £1,000 ($1,600). No one can afford to ignore such amounts of money.

Unforeseen expenses are always a major problem, so let's pick up as many as possible in advance. Not that easy when you're just starting a new business, but as you come across another expense category, add it in to your list. Leave your own living expenses out of this, at the moment we're looking at purely business expenses. By all means do a home budget as well, separately.

Your budget is done in advance, for a year at a time. This means that some figures will be estimates, but these will be amended as they become more clear. One useful tip is to make sure that you have all the *types* of expense, the headings, down on paper. Leave memory out of this, any figure work must always be done on paper, and preferably with a calculator. I repeat, on paper, with a calculator, it's very important. Even better, use a spreadsheet program if you have a computer. You can get freebie spreadsheets from PC magazines, you only need a simple, basic spreadsheet for this work. The layout is the same whether on a computer or on paper, and we'll show you how to go about it, using the sample set of figures shown for the first year of a reading practice.

BUDGET: JANUARY - DECEMBER 2000

	JAN	FEB	MAR	APR	MAY	JUN	JUL	AUG	SEP	OCT	NOV	DEC	TOTALS
INCOME													-
Festivals		377			420				380				1,177
Lectures	90			120			75				75		360
Radio	75		50				50						175
Readings	250	750	1,270	1,800	2,260	2,450	1,800		2,600	2,850	2,350	275	18,655
Other		20											20
TOTALS:	415	1,147	1,320	1,920	2,680	2,450	1,925	-	2,980	2,850	2,425	275	20,387
EXPENSES													-
Adverts	295	50	150	50	295	50	50	50	295	150	50		1,485
Bus. cards	45					45				45			135
Newspapers	18	18	18	18	18	18	18	18	18	18	18	18	216
Petrol	85	45	50	75	45	50	50	45	80	55	45	45	670
Phone			150			234			175			199	758
Stationery	97		25	10	5	5	20	30	5	10	10		217
(etc.)													-
Other	27	15	15	30	25	15	20	10		15	10		182
TOTALS	567	128	408	183	388	417	158	153	573	293	133	262	3,663
INC. - EXP:	-152	1,019	912	1,737	2,292	2,033	1,767	-153	2,407	2,557	2,292	13	16,724
Bal. c/forward		-152	867	1,779	3,516	5,808	7,841	9,608	9,455	11,862	14,419	16,711	
Running balance:	-152	867	1,779	3,516	5,808	7,841	9,608	9,455	11,862	14,419	16,711	16,724	

Convert all your categories into monthly figures, like the news-paper example. You don't have to be exact down to the last penny, in fact keep the decimals out of the picture, they aren't necessary. We have used only a few expense categories in our example, to keep things simple. You will have quite a few more in real life.

One major point to note in our example budget is that both January and August show a negative figure for net income (income minus expenses). In August, during the school holidays, readings are scarce and it is probably a good time to go on holiday yourself. So there's no income shown. Some expenses continue, and they may be much higher than we've shown. This shows clearly how important it is to have money saved up for these bad patches, so it's very important not to spend everything you earn from your readings, but to put away as much as you can right from the start. Keep doing this until you have enough of a cushion to tide you over these bad patches.

A sound target to aim for is to save up enough money to cover all your expenses for six months, and to put that into a separate savings or deposit account, and not to touch that money except in the event of dire emergency. Sure, it will take some time to get such an amount saved up, but work on it as a priority, and put *something* away each time you earn anything, even though at first it may be just a few coins at a time.

This kind of record keeping combines a budget with running totals, which gives you a cashflow forecast as well. Just update the numbers as time goes on, to show your actual income and expenditure, which will help you to spot problem areas before they get out of hand. If reading income starts to drop, then you may need to put out more adverts, and / or reduce your fees a little. If certain expense categories get too high, then you may need to look carefully at any nonessential costs and prune them vigorously.

Looking at our example, you can see how much easier it is to be aware of possible tight periods, and to prepare for them in advance. It is also very satisfying to think that the next year's figures should be much higher, once your practice is well-established.

Fluctuations in the flow of clients

During the run up to Christmas, most people need every penny that they can lay their hands on, and this seems to be the case even in areas where the community is not predominantly Christian. Most clients are female and it is the women who make the physical and financial effort to make a family Christmas a success. Even if such women do have money to spare, they suspend their usual worries and cares until after the holidays when they have time to think about them once more. This means that for all Readers, business usually drops off badly from around the last week in November until some time after the holidays.

Another slow time occurs in the UK during June, July and August - just before and during the family holiday season. Women are not usually as interested in sport as men, but a large number of women follow tennis, which means that in the UK many females are glued to their television sets in June during the Wimbledon fortnight.

There must be similar sporting or annual events in other countries that divert the attention of women. In the southern hemisphere, normal family holiday times are at some other time than the traditional July and August ones of the northern hemisphere, and there too, these slow periods must be taken into account by the Reader.

Think about such periods in your own country. Astrologers can do well in the New Year because some clients feel a need for an annual astrological update at that time of the year, but in general, Readers wait until after their clients have received a month or two's wages and have paid off their Christmas and New Year bills.

Times of optimism and pessimism

The optimism and pessimism in the heading to this piece are the ones that affect clients rather than Readers. There is a mass mood that affects clients which seems to dictate the number and type of clients that contact you at different times of the year. As we have just mentioned, the run up to Christmas and the holiday period itself is a very poor time of the year for business due to the pervading feelings of optimism, the party season and the pleasures of shopping for presents. A client who phones you directly before, after or even during Christmas is bound to be in a state of utter crisis and in such cases it is usually best to suggest that the caller contacts the Samaritans rather than you.

Clients don't need you at optimistic and busy times, such as the run up to Christmas or in the weeks preceding their family holidays, but after these events when life settles down again they will be more receptive to the idea of paying you a visit.

This is even more the case if a dream holiday or an impossibly optimistic view of Christmas turns out to be a flop or worse. The moral of all this is that you can expect your income to fluctuate, and that if you have any sense you will keep some extra money by for the Christmas and pre-holiday lull.

Even during so-called busy times of the year, there are weeks when the phone doesn't ring or worse still, when a string of clients who have made bookings simply fail to turn up. Sometimes this phenomenon is just the way it goes, but there can be less obvious reasons for such a drop-off in trade. You may have hiked your prices, and your charges may now be little too high. If this is the case, drop your prices back down a little and see if that makes a difference.

You may have been overworking and your own Spiritual guides may decide that you need a break. While this is irritating, it is almost a case of "mother knows best", and you can only really go with this particular flow and enjoy the break. If business remains slow after a couple of weeks or so, you will have to review everything that you are doing to see if there is anything you can do to improve matters.

Psychic self-defence

It is just possible that you are being blocked, either by a jealous person or by a spiritual entity. In a normal business book, such a suggestion would sound absolutely crazy, but in our world we know that such things are possible. Fortunately, there are steps that you can take to improve even this nasty condition, and the following ideas may help:

- Treat yourself to a book on Feng Shui and do what you can to improve the energy flow around your place of work. Concentrate on the flow of money energy out of your doors or windows. Look closely at your session seating arrangements or the actual spot where money changes hands, and see if there is anything you can do to improve matters.
- If you think that a person is blocking your progress, do a meditation that involves surrounding yourself with mirrors that will let in the good vibes and keep out the bad ones.
- Fill your premises with "white" light by imagining a light being drawn down from the sky and filling every inch of your home.
- Make a talisman for yourself to bring good luck and prosperity (or ask a friend to buy one for you), and meditate upon this to bring business your way.
- Ask your Spiritual guides for help.

If none of the above solutions help, ask around for someone who professionally handles such problems and make an appointment to see them for a psychic clearance.

Go by reference if you can; if you know anyone who has had a successful psychic clearance, then you are more likely to expect a successful result yourself from that Reader.

If you have a master around your area who can do a Kabbalistic ritual to clear bad vibes, ask him/her to help. You should have little difficulty in finding someone suitable in the USA, but in other countries you may have to hunt around.

If all else fails, consider packing the job in and opening a chicken farm!

Why a chicken farm? Well, this is always Jan's answer whenever he becomes totally fed up with some particularly awkward job that he is working on.

Sasha's mother, Frances Shulman, had a pretty heavy workload during her life, as she ran her own engineering factory making everything from wiring equipment to motor parts, radio and TV parts, and even space and defence items. Her dream was to work in a bread shop with nothing more to consider than picking the right loaf from the shelf and counting out small change.

Sasha's dream is to go back to a previous job where she worked in a typing pool specialising in typing invoices. How restful! How free from anxiety!

RECORD KEEPING AND THE TAX MAN

How long to keep your records – keeping your diary records – sample records – do you need an accountant – income tax, **VAT & National Insurance** – fiddles – tax avoidance – tax deductible expenses – setting household expenses against tax – wot, no receipts? – things you can't claim – things you can partially claim – don't be afraid to communicate – finally...

If the idea of bookkeeping strikes icy fingers of fear into your heart, don't let it. Our simple advice will show you just how valuable all this is, and we will even show you how to go about it in a simple way that will suit most circumstances. If you really can't cope with figure work or record keeping, find someone else who can, and do something for them in exchange that they can't do or that they hate doing. How about swapping a friend's ironing or car-maintenance in exchange for looking after your books? Also take a visit to your local tax office, as they will happily help and advise you. Another good idea is to get a self-employed friend to help you. Jan and I helped our daughter, Helen, to set up a system for her self-employed electrician husband, Riccardo.

Your bookkeeping can be very simple or fairly comprehensive, depending upon the scale of your operations, but your basic need is to make a note of what money comes in, what goes out, and where your outgoings go. The simplest method of all is to buy two note books, one for your income and one for your expenses. Note down all the money that comes in, showing the date, the amount and what you did to earn it. Now comes the most important financial thing that we have to say in the whole of this book, and that is, KEEP RECEIPTS FOR EVERYTHING THAT YOU BUY!! We can't stress this firmly enough, in fact we suggest that you have this engraved on your heart, or that you make a cross-stitch sampler of it to hang in your loo. Keep a note of all your expenses, but do ensure that you have a receipt for each expense item as proof.

Whether your Consultancy is your only job or whether you also have a proper job elsewhere, as a partially or wholly self-employed person, you can put an amazing number of expenses down in your books, which can be set against your tax bill. This is not to suggest that a new bra, a set of saucepans or a new fishing rod is likely to be tax deductible, but you will be surprised when you learn just what is! It is no good telling your accountant or the tax man that you spent money on such and such unless you can prove it, so please, right from day one, keep all receipts!

How long do you need to keep your records for?

Legally, you need to keep your records in the UK for six years but it is probably best to keep them forever. The requirement varies from country to country, but a phone call to your income tax / Inland Revenue department will easily give you the information you need. You can buy archive boxes at any stationers, and then dump the old records in these and shove them up into the loft, but don't forget to get them down again when you move house.

Keeping your diary records

If you ever have the extreme bad luck to be investigated by the tax department, they will want to see your appointment diaries so that they can match the number of clients you have seen to the amount of money you have declared. Such diaries must be kept for six years along with your books. If you are in not in the habit of declaring the full amount of your income in your books, your diaries will catch you out nicely, landing you with a backdated tax bill that will require a second mortgage to pay off. Many pop singers, film stars and successful artists have been caught out in this way. If a huge tax bill does come, this never happens when times are good, but always well after the gravy train has come to a halt and when it is very hard to find the money.

Sample record-keeping
A sample of the simplest form of record-keeping

Income:

1999	Folio No.	Description	Amount
1st Jan	01	Reading	40.00
4th Jan	02	Reading	40.00
5th Jan	03	Talk at local club	25.00
7th Jan	04	Reading	40.00
10th Jan	05	Local radio program	20.00
12th Jan	06	Reading	40.00
20th Jan	07	Day at psychic fair	250.00
Total:			**455.00**

Expenses

1999	Folio No.	Description	Amount
1st Jan	01	Diary	3.00
3rd Jan	02	Tapes for tape recorder	10.00
4th Jan	03	Fee for stand at psychic fair	100.00
5th Jan	04	Stationery	2.50
7th Jan	05	Postage stamps	10.00
9th Jan	06	Phone Bill	60.00
11th Jan	07	A book	6.99
11th Jan	08	Bus ticket	0.60
Total:			**193.09**

The reason for the folio number is so that you can link what you write in your book to each receipt - this is called cross referencing.

The way to deal with receipts is dead easy, you simply number each receipt with the same folio number that you give it in your book. Small receipts can be stapled one below the other on to a piece of A4 paper with two or three on a page. This method makes life easy and it will reduce your accountant's charges. It also makes it easy for you to locate a particular receipt later on if you have a query about it. People talk about keeping receipts in shoe-boxes but believe me, the paper and lever arch file method is far superior.

Don't forget to get a receipt for your note books, your lever arch file (or use an old one that someone else is throwing out) and don't forget to get receipts for your paper, your hole puncher and your staples! You will soon get into the habit of keeping records in this way, and if you ever go into another kind of business, you will already have learned a valuable lesson. If your business grows, you will need to analyse your income and expenditure. If this is getting a bit beyond you, we suggest that you either find a self-employed friend and ask them to show you what they do, or look around your locality for an evening class on basic bookkeeping.

Whatever level of record-keeping you go in for, always fill in the date of any transaction, who it is for or who it is from, give it a folio number and then the total amount. If you then analyse (separate out) your various transactions, you will need a special bookkeeping book that has separate columns for you to use in your analysis. You can then separate out your costs and put the amounts down again under the relevant column. If you are really organised, you can do all this on a computer using a spreadsheet or an accounts software package.

Sample analysis of expenses

Date	Supplier	No	Total	Travel	Stationery	Postage
4 Jan.	Bloggs garage	01	30.00	30.00		
7 Jan.	W H Smith	02	3.75		3.75	
10 Jan.	Train ticket	03	12.00	12.00		
14 Jan.	W H Smith	04	75.00		75.00	
20 Jan.	Postage	05	7.50			7.50
Totals:			128.25	42.00	78.75	7.50

Once you have analysed this lot, take each month at a time and total up all the columns. The amounts in the columns that have been separated out should all add up to the same as the total column, which acts as a double-check.

> **Tips**
> This kind of record-keeping will cut down your account-
> ancy bill by a huge amount.
> It will show you at a glance what you are spending your
> money on.
> If you use the same method for your incoming monies, this
> will show where the bulk of them come from.
> Set aside a particular time - say once a fortnight and do it
> religiously.

If your income and outgoings are not that great, a simple list of incoming and outgoing monies will be enough, but if your business takes off, you will need to do this kind of analysis.

If this is too much of a chore for you, then find someone with a lot of Virgo or Capricorn on their natal charts who just loves to do books, and then offer to do something for them in exchange, that they find difficult. Perhaps your friend would love you to bake a cake for them once in a while, or maybe you could give them a nice break by taking their children out for the afternoon.

Do you need an accountant?

If you are operating in the UK or in the USA, you will have to fill in self-assessment tax forms, so an accountant may be necessary. If you get those nasty little forms from the DSS and you do have an accountant, all you need to do is to give the DSS your National Insurance number and the name and address of your accountant.

If you do everything yourself, including your self-assessment forms, it will be up to you to furnish accounts and to take your books along to the Social Security offices. You are the best judge of what you can handle without professional help.

Can you have a business of this kind and also have a legitimate job?

You can have a full or part time job and also run a business on the side, but consult your local Department of Social Security and/or your tax office to see how you should go about this. If you are not in the UK, you will have to find out what your local scene is, but to our knowledge, there is usually no problem as long as the taxman is kept in the picture (and thus gets his cut!). If you phone or go to see the officials concerned and ask for help, they are usually happy to advise you. Even if you don't have an accountant, you can make an appointment with one and pay for his/her time and advice on a one-off basis.

Income tax, VAT and National Insurance in a little more detail

The organisations that you really shouldn't try to fool are the Department of Social Security (now called the Contributions Agency), the Customs and Excise people (for business people, this means the VAT office) and the Inland Revenue. If you are working in Britain, as soon as you are up and running as a self-employed person, you must apply to the DSS to pay your National Insurance contributions.

The Post Office is a good source of informative leaflets, and you can send off to your DSS office for their very clear booklet. There are different levels of contribution and if you earn very little, your contribution can be reduced or even temporarily set aside.

If you are not operating in the UK, you will need advice on your local situation.

As a self employed consultant in the UK, you may be able to roll forward losses or your start-up expenditure from one year to reduce your tax bill the following year. Once again, check your local situation. Frankly, in these days of self-assessment, a decent accountant can save you time, worry, aggravation and money, so if your business is going to grow beyond the pin-money stage, the money you spend on this is a worthwhile investment.

VAT

At the time of writing in the UK, your business will need to be turning over £51,000 per annum for you to qualify for VAT registration, and if things are that good for you, the chances are that you are very well established in business and that you already have an accountant.

Fiddles

If yours is a cash business, it is easy to slip money into your own pocket without declaring it, but there are drawbacks to this.

Firstly, you may want to go to your bank to raise money for some item such as a computer or a large tape-recorder, and if you haven't shown a reasonable income on your books, how is the bank manager supposed to believe that you will be able to pay them back? In such a case, they will refuse the loan.

Secondly, don't fiddle the Inland Revenue, the DSS (now called the Contributions Agency), the Council Tax people, the VAT or any other official body, because they will find out. When this happens, you will have to repay what you owe, as well as a possible fine, and you may even end up with a criminal record.

Remember that your clients can inadvertently shop you, so pay up if you want to sleep soundly at night. If you take note of the suggestions that follow this section, you will be able to keep your tax bills down to an absolute minimum - not by tax evasion but by tax avoidance. Tax avoidance is quite legitimate.

Avoidance of unnecessary taxation

If you are into meditating or chanting you will find this exercise easy, if you are not, then try this anyway. Visualise a nasty complicated tax form, learn the following mantra by heart, relax in a prone position (in the bath perhaps), and recite to yourself twenty times over, at least once a week...

"Keep all receipts, keep all receipts, keep all receipts, keep all receipts..."

This form of transcendental meditation will lower your blood pressure, slow your heart rate, keep lines off your face, keep hair on your head and it will definitely improve a saggy bottom. Well, perhaps not entirely, but it will save you a fortune!

Do your bookkeeping at least once a fortnight, because if you regularly allow more time than this to elapse, you will lose track of what you are doing. The first thing you need to do is to sort out your papers into income and expenses, and then deal with each book in turn. The number of items that you can put against tax is incredible, and you can save a fortune by being canny with your purchases and receipts. Frankly, anything that can even vaguely be deemed a business expense will often do, and the following list of ideas may help you to see where tax savings can be made. If you do accidentally make an invalid claim, your accountant will usually spot it and leave it out of the equation.

Tax deductible expenses

The following list covers expenses that are, to our knowledge, deductible at the time of writing in the UK. Local conditions may differ. Wherever you live in the world, take a photocopy of this list along with you to your accountant or your tax office and ask them to add to it and / or delete items as necessary.

- Travel by public transport. Keep all tickets, including bus tickets! If your train tickets disappear into an automatic machine, keep a vague note of how much you spend per week on train travel. Ask taxi drivers for a receipt.

Part cost of buying and running a car. (Ask you Inland Revenue Department or your accountant for details).

- Hotel bills.
- Stationery items, office paraphernalia and all such bits and pieces,
- Books of any kind, maybe even those that are not directly related to your work. Who can say what books you may need to read for research purposes?
- Magazines and papers.
- Your computer and everything to do with it. Also any other such office machinery.

- Office services. For example, if you have some photocopying done, get a receipt.

Your accountancy fees are also deductible - claim them!

- Phone bills of all kinds, even phone cards.
- Tape recorder, tapes, batteries.
- If you broadcast, you can put part of the cost of your television and video against tax. Small radios, etc. may be completely deductible. It is unlikely that the tax-man would require proof of this, but if you keep a video of any programmes that you appear on, the proof will be there for all to see.
- Dry cleaning, ironing (small amounts may be acceptable).
- Subscription fees for any societies or unions that you join.
- Anything you pay others to do for you in connection with your work. If you farm jobs out to others, get them to give you an invoice on headed paper or a little signed note to show their charges to you.
- Coffee, tea, milk, biscuits, loo rolls and some cleaning costs that result from you having people in for readings.
- Tarot cards, crystal ball, dowsing rods and anything else to do with your work.

Setting some of your household expenses against tax

If you are in the UK and if you work from home, you will be allowed to offset a small amount against your tax bill to cover a proportion of your consultancy room costs. Your accountant will advise you on this. The amount is actually not very large, but every little bit helps. This situation applies whether you own your own home or rent it.

Wot, no receipts?

In the UK and probably elsewhere, you are allowed to put a certain amount of expense against tax without having to produce receipts. You can't be too fanciful, but a reasonable sounding amount is acceptable. The following items are typical:

The coins that you pour into parking meters (in London, this can be a considerable expense).

Magazines and other publications to do with your work.

Cleaning, ironing, occasional office help in exchange for small amounts of cash.

Things that you cannot claim for

In the UK, the only trades or professions that qualify for tax relief on clothing are those where it can be proved that the clothes can never be used for anything other than work. Such items might include a lawyer's wig, a miner's lamp, a diver's wet-suit or a stripper's outfit. There was a case in the papers fairly recently in which female lawyers claimed that their drab black suits and white blouses were only suitable for work and that they wouldn't be worn for any other purposes, and this was thrown out by the tax man! Those who do bar work or pub work and who wear their own clothes are allowed to put dry cleaning against tax, but not the clothes themselves. The same applies to Readers.

Subsistence in the form of food and drink is not tax deductible in the UK, except by travelling representatives. Sue Lilly suggests that if you are away from home you choose a hotel that offers bed and breakfast because this will come under the category of hotel expenses and this is deductible. She says that Readers should stuff themselves with breakfast in the hopes that this will keep them going for several hours, thereby saving on the expense of buying lunch. If you are one of those Readers who can't work on a very full stomach, perhaps you could arrange for the hotel to give you a doggy bag!

Your local laws and local situations must be studied in order to get all such tax matters right. For example, in the USA you could possibly put a suite of furniture, your children's education, money donated to charity and the upkeep of an expensive lover against tax, while the Inland Revenue in the UK is far more parsimonious! Also, in the USA remember that tax and other laws vary from one state to another, so get advice for the position in your own location and if you move, get a new accountant in your new area.

It is really not possible for us to give specific advice for any country besides the one we live in; it would be impossible for us to stay current on changes in even one other country, except on a full-time basis. The book would never be up-to-date for long, and furthermore, this book is not intended to be a legal, medical or any other kind of "bible"; in many countries including the USA, you can't (and we don't try to) render any professional services in a book such as this one. You have to approach the relevant professionals for whichever type of service you need, and we recommend you do so anyway because that's the way to get the best advice possible.

Things that you can partially claim for

You may not be able to claim the whole cost of buying and running a vehicle against tax (in the UK), but you will certainly be able to claim a part of it. You may have difficulty in claiming the whole of your telephone bill against tax in some areas, and if you have two lines, you may only be able to deduct the cost of the one you use for business. Phone cards may be wholly or partially deductible. If in doubt about any of this, take this chapter along to your local tax office and let them go through it for you. If you discover anything we have left out, please let us know!

You can see from the suggested list that many things that can be reasonably legitimately classed as helping you to do your job can be tax deductible. This is generally the case in most countries, but as always, do check the specific parameters in your country.

Overseas travel can be used as a tax-deductible expense if your journey is purely for business purposes. For example, going overseas for a business conference or for research purposes. You cannot claim for other people travelling with you (unless they are clearly required for business reasons) or for what is obviously a holiday - with or without your family!

If you want to earn money abroad by giving readings, teaching or giving lectures, you will need work permits, visas, tax experts in the country you intend to work in, and a whole host of other exasperating stuff. If you do the odd reading while on holiday and some grateful person buys you dinner in exchange, even the tax man would advise you to keep this fact to yourself.

Don't be afraid to communicate

Sue made a comment that Jan and I totally agree with, and that is to speak up. Tax officials are approachable and helpful and if you don't have an accountant they will help you to fill in your self-assessment forms for you. Ask your local officials to tell you what part of a car, television, phone bill, household overheads or anything else is legally deductible; they will be happy to tell you.

Tips

Another of Sue's tips is that if you take private lessons or if you consult a guru in the UK, you should get a receipt for any money that you pay, as this is tax deductible. A tax deductible Guru? Well, why not?

Finally

Don't fiddle. Be honest. Declare your earnings and pay your way. Self-employment is hard enough without having to worry about tax irregularities as well!

Sasha's stories...

A few years ago I had the usual new business visit from the VAT man and he turned out to be a mine of information on VAT claims and general taxation matters. He pointed out a number of things that I had never considered claiming for.

Neither of us are tax experts, but Jan's 31 years in the world of banking and finance, and Sasha's lifetime of self-employment mean that we know the scene in general terms. However, we strongly advise you to consult officials and accountants in your own locality because they will know the laws that apply in your country. Whatever you do, don't allow a situation to drift along without being properly dealt with, as you could find yourself being asked to pay back taxes, which if you had kept receipts and records, might never have been necessary in the first place.

READERS, CLIENTS AND CIVILIANS

Clients & civilians – being special – hostility – more advice on handling social occasions – take a break

The heading to this section may seem daft, but you will see what we are getting at as we go along. The topic we are focusing on here relates to appropriate and inappropriate times for working or for talking about your work.

Clients and civilians

The definition of a client is someone who consults you, either for a reading, for lessons or for some other legitimate purpose, and for which they pay an agreed fee. We have pinched the term "civilian" from show business. It is the term that showbiz folk use to describe those who do not work in "the business". Civilians have preconceived ideas about our work that are usually totally divorced from reality. Jan and I are sure that we are all just as ignorant in our turn about a film star's work and lifestyle.

Being special

If your psychological motivation for becoming a Reader is to be seen as being special, then talking about your work to all and sundry will give you just what you need. Whether this will make you a good Reader or not is hard to judge, but it certainly will get you noticed.

Sasha's stories...

Several years ago, an acquaintance of mine who is a rather silly Aries gentleman, took up the Tarot and began to give readings at his home in the evenings after he had finished his normal day's work. He had a definite aptitude for Tarot reading, but his attitude was an unusual one. Not only did he talk about his Tarot expertise at every opportunity, but if encouraged by the slightest interest (especially from a woman), he whipped out his cards faster than a stage magician showing off his favourite trick.

On one occasion, this man and I went to a local pub for a drink and a bit of lunch. When we arrived, I nipped straight into the loo and when I came out and walked up to the bar, I was astounded at what I saw. My friend had his Tarot cards spread out on the bar and he was trying to give the barmaid a Tarot reading. This was quite something to see, because although it was a little before lunch time and the bar wasn't yet too busy, one or two customers were beginning to drift up to be served. In between dodging backwards and forwards to deal with them, the barmaid kept swivelling her eyes round towards my friend and straining to hear what he had to say. My pal was in heaven because he had achieved his lifetime ambition of capturing the wholehearted attention of an attractive female stranger, whilst at the same time distracting her from her job and the demands and requirements of other men. This man became so overwhelmed with the success of his ploy that the following week, he even pulled out his cards at the supermarket check-out - and this caused even more chaos!

The chances are that if you stick with this business, the feeling of being special will wear off pretty quickly. In party or social situations, you will encounter a number of responses. Some people will be happy to ask a few intelligent questions and leave it at that. Others will press you for an on-the-spot reading or even a complete training course in your subject right there and then. Some really lovely folk will even try to goad you into proving yourself by insinuating that you aren't psychic or that you don't really know anything about graphology or whatever.

Our friend and colleague, Jonathan Dee, tells us that when he is at some social event or other, there is invariably someone who sticks his hand under Jon's nose expecting Jon to read it for him. This, despite the fact that Jon is a famous astrologer and that he doesn't read hands. The public thinks that we can all read hands (whether we can or not) and worse still, that we all want to even when it is quite obvious that we are off duty.

You can exhaust yourself by trying to explain that you are not actually at work any more than any of the other party-goers are, but some pests refuse to understand this and they can get extremely shirty about it. If you are out socially, you are entitled to spend your free time enjoying yourself, and sometimes you have to point this out. There may be occasions when you are perfectly happy to talk about your work, but if you don't feel like it, then don't do it.

As with doctors, lawyers and other professional people, don't be led into giving "quickie" consultations at social events; usually these don't work out well, and you risk getting egg on your face instead of promoting your abilities.

Hostility

You will encounter hostile responses from some people, and there can be a number of motives behind this, some of these having at least a semblance of reason and others that have none at all. You may have the misfortune to find yourself talking to a religious fundamentalist, in which case you have two choices. Either ask your extremist friend to talk about his beliefs while you nod wisely in response, or simply excuse yourself and then find a wickedly large drink and someone else to chat to.

Apart from religious zealots, the worst "anti" folk that Sasha has encountered are astronomers who, fortunately, are few and far between. Astronomers have a fascist hatred of our work, with astrology at the very top of their hate list. Unlike us, astronomers tend to be amateurs who often fancy themselves as scientists. They consider that to be accepted as such, an interest in divination is politically incorrect. This attitude ignores such facts as the current discussions between the Astrological Association of Great Britain and two UK universities, as to which one will be chosen to create a Chair in Astrology. Acceptance of astrology is fast becoming politically correct, whether stick-in-the-mud types like it or not.

Sociologists can also be hostile, but anybody who is in the counselling game is likely to be very much on our side. These comments are generalisations of course, because civilians can be hostile, accepting or anything else depending upon their natures. We have found sympathetic meteorologists, financial analysts and bank managers, business executives and even some astronomers who are closet astrologers, clairvoyants and so on.

Some civilians are jealous of our talents, while many think that we earn a fortune off the backs of silly or unfortunate people who pay enormous sums to consult us. Sasha remembers one occasion when an accountant lectured her on the fact that she should be giving her time and her skills away for nothing. Sasha suggested that he should try doing this first, before telling someone else to give up their livelihood.

More advice on handling social occasions

It can be unwise to be seen to be doing business at a social occasion so don't arrange specific appointments and don't discuss your schedules or your fees. If someone shows a genuine interest in consulting you, simply hand them a card and tell them to ring you at a later date when you will be happy to discuss details with them.

Take a break

You need to do things that are unrelated to your work to create a balance in your life, so take the time to socialise with friends, play sports, go on a shopping spree, have a holiday, enjoy your hobbies and play with your children or grandchildren. Spend time with the family, gossip with a pal on the phone, watch the telly, read books that are unrelated to your work and - in short - get a life!

Chapter 23

A POT-POURRI

If you see something bad in a reading – be kind to your self – the garden party – further dead-loss situations – mildly hostile clients – getting it just right – an exciting tale – Nostradamus & company...

Here are some final comments, stray pieces of advice and a few more stories from ourselves and from the gang of gypsies, tramps and thieves who have contributed so much to this book. The following items don't fall into any special category but they are all interesting and some are very important indeed, so read on.

What do you say if you see something bad in a reading?

The fact is, there is no easy answer to this one. If we simply say to you "it all depends," that isn't going to be much help, so let us list some ideas that may help you when you are faced with this particularly nasty dilemma.

- Never, never, never give a client bad news in order to dramatise a reading or to make yourself appear more interesting and exciting as a Reader. If your ego needs this kind of boost, get out of this business immediately - and stay out of it!
- Ask yourself if you are absolutely sure that what you think you are seeing is right. If you are not one hundred per cent sure that you are right about a potentially nasty situation, water it down.

- Try to ascertain whether your client can cope with bad news or not, and then assure him that you are fallible and things may not turn out to be half as bad as the reading seems to suggest.
- If your client is neurotic, don't hand him bad news, he won't be able to handle it.

In the very rare event that you come across a client who you think is going to die in the near future, keep this to yourself. Most disasters can be averted and it is often worth a client's while to be advised of them - indeed, that may be the reason why the client's own Spiritual guides brought him to you in the first place. But death is the ultimate act of God, and there is little that is useful in being given a date for such an event; it is far more likely to cause the client constant worry, sleepless nights and perhaps even lead to rash actions he would otherwise never have contemplated. Some Indian astrologers like to give their clients death dates but we can't see any useful purpose in this.

Once in a very blue moon, you will be faced with a client who knows himself that he is dying. If you don't want to let him talk to you about his situation or if you feel ill-equipped to deal with it, suggest that he finds a bereavement counsellor to talk to. If you want to go ahead with the session, just let your client talk his heart out and call upon your Spiritual guides to put the words into your mouth that will give the poor man what he needs.

Be kind to yourself

We have already written about a series of events concerning demanding clients, but here is yet another story that Jonathan Dee passed on to us. A woman phoned Jonathan when he has just returned from the funeral of a loved-one. This client wanted to see him there and then, and she wouldn't take no for an answer. When he told her his situation she answered, "What does that matter? I need a reading and I need it now!" Jon promptly told the caller to visit a taxidermist.

Sasha's stories...
The garden party

A woman who had been recommended by a client phoned me and insisted that she come for an appointment the following weekend. I didn't want to work at that time, so I suggested that she leave it for a week or two and then give me a ring. On the following Sunday afternoon, I was sitting in my garden having a lovely alfresco tea with my family and some friends when the doorbell rang. My daughter went to see who it was, and a few moments later she walked back into our garden followed by a tall, good looking woman who had a school-aged child in tow. This lady marched up the garden and stood in front of me demanding that I abandon my visitors and my family and attend to her there and then. I politely but firmly saw her off my premises.

Further dead loss situations

Some clients are in such an emotional mess that nobody can sort them out. Such folk must turn to counselling. If they are addicted to drink or drugs or anything else, or if they are living with an addict, they must go to the appropriate organisation. All these organisations are listed towards the front of any telephone directory and all details can also be found at the public library.

Mildly hostile clients

A surprising number of clients show hostility at the start of an appointment because they are nervous and unsure of what to expect, but these clients soon settle down and warm to you once they see that they can trust you. Others are angry, hostile and even dangerous due to the unhappy and confusing state of their lives at the time of the reading. A little hostility can be tolerated, but if it is more than that, show the client the door. Wherever you are working, and especially if you are in your own home, you don't have to put up with bad treatment.

If any client starts to act in a sexy way or starts to say anything that you feel is inappropriate, tell them to go. Of course, if you really fancy them ... you can arrange to meet them socially some other time. Just remember that this is rarely a good idea, and mixing business with pleasure is never a good idea.

Getting it just right...

Jonathan Dee tells a lovely story of the day he was analysing a client's chart and noticed that the client had an afflicted Neptune in the fourth house. The fourth house represents the past, often the home and family environment, and sometimes one of the parents. Neptune indicates a love of water and/or a love of drink. Jonathan's intuition suddenly kicked in and he casually asked his client, "Was your father by any chance a drunken sailor?"

"No," answered the client, "he was a drunken swimming bath attendant!"

An exciting tale

Here is one story that I shall never forget. An attractive man of about 30 came to see me and he brought an equally attractive girlfriend along with him to hear what I had to say. This chap whom I shall call Kevin, requested an astrology reading. I was delighted to find that he knew a fair bit about astrology, because this always makes a reading easier and more enjoyable for me.

As I worked my way through the natal chart, I began to see that Kevin lived an exciting life. I could see a deep interest in criminal matters and I suggested that he might be a policeman. Kevin answered in the negative. I tried him with suggestions of forensic work, a paramilitary life or even a job as a private detective. No, it wasn't any of these. I laughingly suggested that Kevin must be a criminal — and this time he concurred! After I had recovered from my surprise, I amplified my comments by suggesting that he worked at a high-level of crime and once again, Kevin agreed. Kevin then went on to tell me that he was a "peterman", which is a safe-cracker, and as such, the very top of the criminal heap.

At the time of the reading, Kevin had apparently come to the end of a series of bank robberies and it looked as though the police were closing in on some of his accomplices. Kevin then told me he was worried because - as he told me in his cockney accent - "My Plu'o's a bit shitty at the moment". This translated to mean that a couple of planets were badly aspecting Kevin's Pluto. I told him that this was indeed a dodgy situation, but that he shouldn't find himself "grassed-up" by his pals if any of them did get caught, because his Neptune was doing fine. "Thank gawd for that", said Kevin with a sigh of relief, "You can get away with a bad Plu'o but when your Nep-chune's buggered, so are you!".

Nostradamus and company...

Some months ago we received a package in the post from a man in New Zealand, who was trying to sell a book through the Internet. The pages were part of an introduction to a carefully worked astro-logical treatise on the date for the potential end of the world. We each read the dense and heavily academic tract, and we were so impressed with the sources, the arguments and the sheer intellectu-alism of the approach that we found ourselves beginning to think that this guy had a point. However, before we could become too concerned about the impending world's end, we noticed that the date when this was supposed to occur had already passed!

The moral: You can find facts seemingly to back up practically any notion that enters your head... keep personal fantasies away from your work.

WHEN IT ALL GOES WRONG...

When the Reader has it all wrong – common personal or emotional problems – avoiding common practical problems – timing – readings that misfire – client related problems – the plumber – blockages – the wrong kind of reading – dozy clients – foreign clients – clients from hell – it's not over until the fat lady sings – the oversized bosom syndrome – bad news – Veronica – a plate of jelly – can I have the good stuff now, please? – the proof of the pudding – what can be expected from a reading – overdemanding clients – the Royal Marine Bandsman syndrome

To the outsider, to the "civilian", the job of a Reader must look like money for old rope. After all, what is there to it? Throw a few cards, give a vague prediction or two and another happy client floats out the door, and all that remains is to take a pile of money around to the bank. What can go wrong? In our opinion just about everything can go wrong, and in examining the possibilities we have come to the conclusion that the two main areas of potential trouble are the Reader and the client!

When the Reader has it all wrong

The following tale is true and it shows just how important the attitude of a Reader is.

Some years ago, an acquaintance of ours became interested in taking up Tarot reading as an addition to his normal job. This chap definitely had some ability, as he was a good judge of character and he also had a measure of psychic talent, but he made two important mistakes. The first of these was a practical matter and the second was a matter of ideology.

The first mistake was to unleash himself on the public far too soon without doing all those things that we have talked about in previous chapters, such as thoroughly studying his craft, reading extensively and trying out his skills on friends or at school fetes and so on. Our friend plunged directly into the twofold course of inviting clients to visit him at his home and taking himself off to read at a small psychic fair at the earliest opportunity. He fared reasonably well with the clients who consulted him at his home, because he took the time to talk to them and to assess their personalities before plunging into giving them a reading. He was lucky that his clients accepted this approach, but he found that he was spending a couple of hours or more with each client, which was not cost-effective.

When our friend went to his first psychic festival, he found that the clients who attended this event expected a different approach. They wanted to sit in silence while he quickly got into their minds and their lives, and accurately told them what was happening. His lack of training, knowledge or true psychic development meant that he simply couldn't operate in this way, and one reading after another failed. He left the festival without even having taken enough money to pay for his table, and he never did another "gig" of this kind again. Had he persisted, he could have done all right in the end, but he fell at the first real hurdle.

This man's ideological mistake was to take up the work for all the wrong reasons. His first desire was to be seen as being something special, while his second was to tap into what he considered to be a way of earning easy money. His third thought focused upon the notion of a stream of nubile women trotting through his home.

None of these aspirations work, as our friend discovered to his cost. In fact, providence paid him out for his wrong-footed attitude in the most peculiar way, by setting a completely neurotic woman on him, who, having once consulted him, phoned him for guidance morning, noon and night, every day for some months afterwards.

Common personal or emotional problems

You will be off-colour or even unwell at times, or you may simply have an off-day on occasion. This happens to everybody in every kind of job, so don't beat yourself up about it. You may know you are not at your best but try to keep this away from your clients and just get through the day as well as you can. If you really mess up on a particular reading, explain that you are not at your best and don't take the client's money. It is not nice when this kind of thing happens, but it does show that you are human and not a fairground speak-your-weight and fortune-telling machine.

You may have eaten or drunk too much. An over-full stomach can block the workings of some of your chakras, while 'booze' can block everything. One drink can actually improve your performance, but a few of them will mess it up completely. About the only thing you can do here is to drink water during the day, as it will dilute whatever is going on in your stomach.

Fatigue makes it hard for you to concentrate, and if this is the result of a few late nights, cut down your bookings for a few days and get to bed early. If you are overwrought, burned out or temporarily fed up with the job, do something else for a while if you can. It is difficult to concentrate on others when you have problems of your own, and the answer here is probably to cut down on your work for a while until you have sorted out your own life.

Avoiding common practical problems

The best time to start getting a reading on to a good footing is when a prospective client first makes contact with you, and this is likely to be by phone. A client who has been recommended by a friend who has already seen you should know what to expect, but he or she still may require information. A sensible client will ask you about the kind of reading you do, how long this will take, how much you charge and so on.

When a new client contacts you, you should tell him a little of what you do so he can come to you with confidence. If you pick up the fact that the caller needs a different divination from whatever it is that you do, suggest that they go to someone else.

If you know of a colleague who can help your caller, pass the details on. Don't try to force the client's needs to fit into your divination, even if the client is willing to try. You are expected to know better than the client whether or not you can fulfil his needs.

Timing

You will remember from our story at the beginning of this chapter that our unsuccessful Reader's hourly rate was too low due to his taking far too long over each reading. This is a common problem and it can happen to the best Reader. Experience will show you how long you need for a reading and it will also teach you how to speed up your work.

Actors who work regularly on the radio or television tell us that the public become so accustomed to seeing them in their living rooms that they view them as friends; but the actor of course, doesn't know the civilian from Adam. The same thing can occur with a Reader and his clients, especially those who make fairly regular visits. Such a visit is an outing to the client, and given half a chance, he or she will turn it into a half-day gossip session. You may wish to while away a half-day or so in your client's company, perhaps even making lunch or introducing the client to your family.

All that is fine if it is what you want out of your day's work, otherwise simply get the job done and encourage the client to end the session and to go happily on his or her way.

As we have said elsewhere in this book, it is often advisable to group your clients together in the same way that a therapist does as this will discourage lingerers. Remember the candle trick that we mentioned in an earlier chapter if you need help in bringing your sessions to an end.

Readings that misfire

If you are new to this work, you may find that a few readings misfire and that you can't give your client what he or she needs. One or two failed readings now and again are acceptable, but more misses than hits shows that something is wrong, and you must ask yourself whether you are giving the wrong kind of information to your clients. For example, are you keen on health matters while your clients are interested in hearing about their relationships? Are you working as a psychologist when your clients want fortune telling? If this is the case, then your advertising material or the description you give prospective clients about your particular way of work is not right. You may be terribly keen on something that simply doesn't gel with the public, such as a Reader that Sasha once visited who insisted on treating her to a long lecture on the state of the world, UFO's and the nature of Jesus Christ. If you want an audience for your views, try politics instead.

That's about it for Reader-related problems; the rest of this chapter is devoted to our clients and the aggravation that some of them give us. Bear in mind that the vast majority of clients are terrific. They enjoy their session with you, they get something useful out of it and they go on to recommend you to their friends. The examples that we give below are the exception rather than the rule, but all of us meet such clients from time to time, and if nothing else, they give us something to moan about to our colleagues and friends.

Client-related problems

Here are a few typical problems that you are bound to meet sooner or later. The list outlines the problems in general and the remainder of this chapter goes into them in detail. We have illustrated some situations with true stories.

The "no, no, no" syndrome.

Psychic blockages.

The wrong kind of reading.

Ignorant clients.

Those who can't understand a word the Reader is saying.

Crazy clients.

Suicidal clients and those who are in deep emotional pain.

Survey clients.

Plutonic clients.

Every Reader comes up against the occasional client who can't accept what he or she is being told. If the reading is based on something factual, such as astrology or numerology, check whether the data that the client has given you is actually right. It is not impossible for a client to furnish an astrologer with a wrong time of birth, a wrong place of birth and even a wrong date of birth. The upshot of this is that the astrologer finds himself in effect giving the client someone else's reading. The same problem occurs in numerology because if the date of birth is wrong, the whole reading will be wrong. Sometimes the client realises his or her mistake and phones back a day or two later, asking if the Reader can redo the reading - naturally, at the Reader's expense - not theirs!

Spiritual mediums and clairvoyants need some confirmation from their client at various stages of the reading, so that their Spiritual guides can proceed. The Reader does not need chapter and verse from the client, but he does need to know that the client recognises what is being said to them and that the reading is being accepted. Many skilled mediums will actually make a statement such as, "can you accept this?" at points during the procedure before moving on to the next message. If the client is determined to say no at every turn then the reading cannot proceed. There are a couple of possible reasons for a misfire in a reading of this kind, the first being that the Reader might not be giving the messages clearly enough, and if the client is on a different wavelength, he or she simply may not be able to see what the Reader is getting at. The following story is about a very frustrating incident of the "no, no, no" kind.

Sasha's stories...

The plumber

How can I ever forget the case of a woman who consulted me some years ago, who displayed this denial syndrome in a particularly vivid manner. The lady was booked in for a Tarot reading which should have taken no more than forty-five minutes, but in the end I read her cards, her hands, her horoscope and everything else I could think of. I knew that what I was seeing was right despite her denials, and I simply had to prove this to myself - if not to her. I had already worked out her character correctly, I knew she had one child and a good husband and I had correctly stated that she worked as a plumber, which is a very unusual occupation for a woman. This gave me the security of knowing that I had tuned into her pretty well.

I knew for a certainty that the lady plumber was either in, or about to embark upon, an affair with a younger man whom she had met through her work, and that this would break up what appeared to be a perfectly good marriage. The lady plumber denied this emphatically. At long last, I let her leave after charging her only a minimal amount for the partially correct reading. I was pretty well exhausted after this marathon session and I can't deny that I was glad to see her picking up her coat in anticipation of going. As she put her arms into the sleeves of her coat she commented that she had indeed taken a fancy to a younger man who she had met at work, and that it had "crossed her mind" to do something about him. I could cheerfully have clocked her one!

Blockages

Blockages might sound like another plumbing story, but in this case we are talking about psychic blockages. This problem is really bad news for a medium or a channeller, but it is no less dramatic for a Tarot Reader. One odd story that Sasha tells is of a lady for whom Sasha was reading, who told her that the reading was extremely accurate, except for the fact that the events had all occurred forty years previously! Fortunately the client was fascinated by this turn of events, and Sasha had enough skill to "ask" the cards to give another reading that concentrated on the here and now! Tarot is a peculiar divination, because the cards tend to leap upon the nearest event or matter that causes the client to feel strong emotions. Such an event may be in the past, present or future, but it is rare that it is as far back as in this case!

The client's own spiritual guides may block a reading, either because they don't want the client to have a reading at that moment in time or because they want him or her to go to someone other than you. This is hard to accept, but it does sometimes happen. Sometimes the timing is wrong and the blockage will lift a week or so later. A good ploy is to phone a colleague and see if he or she can fit your client in for an emergency reading and then let the client come back to you once again at a later date. Making this kind of effort on behalf of a client always impresses them, and they usually end up visiting both you and your friend on occasion in the future, and they recommend both you and your colleague to their friends.

Sasha's stories...

Some years ago, a lady called Jan came to see me for a Tarot reading and try as I might, I just couldn't make a link with her. In desperation, I asked my daughter Helen who is a total amateur Tarot Reader to come in and see if she could make the link. Helen immediately linked with Jan and ended up taking over the entire session. Despite the fact that Helen told Jan that she was a complete amateur and that she didn't want to be paid for her "work" Jan insisted on paying up. A few weeks later Jan came back to see me, and this time whatever had been blocking us had lifted and the job went perfectly. Perhaps Helen needed to be shown that she could give a competent reading to a perfect stranger? Who knows?

Do bear in mind that there are some people for whom you will never be able to read due to some kind of spiritual incompatibility. Such a phenomenon is very rare but it if does happen, all you can do is to recommend your client to another colleague and leave it at that.

The wrong kind of reading

If you are faced with someone who needs a different kind of job from the type that you offer, refer the client to someone who works in the field that they require. The following story is a nice one, but it all began when my friend, Barbara found herself being given the wrong kind of reading.

Barbara Ellen and John Lindsay

Our lovely friend, Barbara, is an extremely competent clairvoyant, but like all of us, she can't give herself a proper reading. At the point in time when the following event happened, she badly needed one, so she decided to consult a Reader who was a stranger to her for some enlightenment. Barbara consulted the late and much missed John Lindsay. Now John was an excellent palmist and he gave her a truly insightful reading into her character, but he gave her very little guidance about her future, which is what Barbara really needed at that point in her life.

To all intents and purposes the reading was a waste of Barbara's time and money, but she took this situation philosophically. Eventually, Barbara became a good friend of John's, even learning a fair bit of palmistry from him as a result. Thus the whole experience became a net gain rather than a net loss.

Many clients benefit greatly from a sensitive character reading as this can show them how they act and react on an inner level. In the case of a such a client, a good palmistry reading is invaluable, but if what they actually need is healing or a spiritual medium, they may not appreciate this. Sometimes even the wrong kind of reading isn't too great a problem as your client will still benefit from it.

Dozy clients

Some clients are so dozy that they barely understand what a Reader is saying to them. If you are faced with a client like this, avoid talking in any form of symbolic language and just come out with bald black and white statements. If the client is unbelievably dozy, point out that the reading is being tape-recorded and that the client should take the tape home and play it to a friend who will go over it with them. This may sound unbelievable, but it does happen.

Foreign clients

Some clients don't really understand English (or whatever language you are working in) and in this case, once again you simply tell them that you will put their reading on tape while they are sitting there, and that they should take it home and get a friend whose English is better than theirs to go over it with them. Naturally, in this case you won't be able to ask for confirmation of the "can you accept this message" type, as they won't even understand it. Another ploy may be to ask the client to come back again with an interpreter in tow.

Clients from hell

Much as we want to love all our clients, sometimes this is just not possible. Some clients are so unhappy about their personal problems that they try to take their rage and fury out on us. Point out to such a client that you understand that they are in pain, but that there are other more appropriate ways of dealing with this. Suggest counselling, psychotherapy, marriage guidance or something of the ilk, and if they continue to be obstreperous, ask them to leave.

Your client may be crazy! You are not a psychiatrist and you don't have to deal with those who are severely mentally ill, so if you are faced with such a client, turn him or her away as quickly as you can and don't take any money from them. Sasha tells a tale of an elderly female client who was completely crackers and very hostile. Sasha tried to give her a reading and then gave up and asked her to leave. The client then cheerfully commented that three other Readers had also thrown her out!

You are not a mental health worker and you don't need to have this kind of negativity hanging around you.

Your client may be suicidal. Help if you can, otherwise suggest that they phone or visit the Samaritans organisation.

Sasha's stories...

I remember one poor guy who came to see me a few years ago. It was a couple of days after Christmas, his girlfriend had dumped the poor man on Christmas Eve and he was absolutely suicidal. My own Christmas had been bloody awful and I felt in much the same state of mind as he did. I poured each one of us a glass of whisky and made us a coffee and we wept on each other's shoulders for a while. Not professional perhaps but some-times there is a time and a place for daft behaviour.

It's not all over until the fat lady sings

Jonathan Dee tells a wonderful story about a heavily overweight female client who plonked herself down on his sofa-bed and promptly broke it. To his utter amazement, the woman took herself over to a sturdier chair and stared at him in anticipation of her reading with-out saying one word about his broken furniture. Jonathan was lucky not to be working in the USA, as such an event would encourage the client to sue him for causing bruises to her rear end! I believe that one can get insurance for clients' accidents, and perhaps this would be worth some consideration.

The oversized bosom syndrome

Some clients are impossible to please. Consider the following scenario. Your client is female, middle aged and equipped with an oversized bosom which appears to have a life and a character of its own! We can almost hear you thinking, 'What on earth has the size of a woman's bosom got to do with anything?' Well, it hasn't really, but there are a few occasions when a magnificently out-of-control bosom seems to drain common sense from the brain while reducing a woman's capacity for kindness and understanding. We are not the only people to have observed this syndrome, as it is mentioned graphically in Donna Cunningham's excellent book, "Healing Pluto Problems". When you come across this kind of female, expect that her reaction to almost anything that you say will be to cross her arms defensively across her vast mounds, to thrust her lower jaw out and to be ready to disbelieve you or to discredit you at all costs. Such clients tend to have the planet Pluto emphasised in their natal charts.

The woman "way across town"

If you are the same generation as Jan and myself, or if you happen to love old pop music, you will be familiar with the wonderful early Elvis Presley song that goes, "I've got a woman, way across town who's good to me." Well, we have already mentioned the mythical woman way across town who gets away with charging a fortune, and here is another mythical across-town woman whom you can do without.

You may be working away quite happily when your client flabbergasts you by commenting that some Reader over the other side of town was much better than you because she "told her everything". This does nothing for your confidence, and when you get over this slap in the face you will have to analyse your next actions. Before you get into a complete flap and lose your temper with the client, try asking her (this client is always a woman) to tell you in detail what was different about the reading. Better still, if the across-town reader taped the reading, ask if your client could possibly bring the tape in for you to listen to. Obviously you can't take any money for this client's reading. It may even be a good idea to offer to pay your client's expenses in making a second visit to you, because it would be well worth the trouble and expense to discover just what is going on here.

If the client cooperates with you, you may discover that a) the across-town Reader *really is* much better than you or b) that the across-town Reader has made a point of telling the client those things that she most wants to hear. At least try to discover the name and address of this Reader so that you can consult her yourself, because you will then confirm that the Reader is either a "bull-duster" or that she really is good. If the standard between her readings and yours is genuinely different, you may have to take some more training in order to improve your own performance. At the very worst, you will find out where to go for a good reading when you want one for yourself!

If your client refuses to elaborate upon what the mysterious "everything" that she has been told by the other paragon of a reader actually was, and if she can't or won't let you listen to a tape, and she can't or won't pass on the Reader's details, then all you can do is to admit failure on this one, refuse to take the client's money, write the episode off to experience and put it behind you.

Bad news

The public and the media love to ask us what we do when we see something bad. We have covered this topic in more detail in another chapter, but there are times when you can say something in all innocence that upsets or shakes a client in an unexpected manner. The following two stories illustrate the point very nicely.

Sasha's stories...

Veronica

My first comment to Veronica as I laid down some cards, was that she was in a muddle at work, at which point the poor woman promptly burst into tears and became extremely distressed. I gave her a box of tissues and made her a cup of tea. I then suggested that we forget the reading for a moment, and that Veronica unburden herself about her problem.

Veronica was a tall, slim, pleasant looking but very reserved woman of about 37 years of age. She was quite obviously the type who had never developed the confidence for dating, and her spinsterish manner had not attracted male attention. No doubt she had long since accepted this fate. Now, however, things had changed in a big way! While others of her age had broadened out and lost the bloom of youth, Veronica's tall, slim, dark Virgoan appearance was looking good by comparison.

Veronica's parents had both died during the previous year, leaving her with a house and quite a bit of money. Suddenly the gentle, quiet and comfortably off Veronica had become extremely interesting to the opposite sex. Not one but three men at her place of work had suddenly become switched on to her presence. These ageing Romeos had probably had their share of good-looking, socially competent but demanding women, and they had begun to see that living with a nice, quiet, considerate lady, who happened to have a good "wedge" in the bank, could make a pleasant change. I can't even begin to comment about their thoughts on the prospect of waking up this virginal sleeping beauty!

The three men had entered a fierce competition for Veronica's company, and after so many sterile years, this confused and frightened her. Not having had played the dating game before, Veronica was even less aware of the way men's minds worked than those long-married ladies who suddenly find themselves widowed or divorced and back in the marketplace once again.

Veronica and I talked things over and I tried to explain the thinking behind the three men's actions. Veronica decided to reject all three of these chancers, but to use the experience to learn a little about men and about courtship. The realisation that at long last she had much to offer a man was an important turning point for her, and she decided to give this some thought and possibly to open herself up to genuine offers of decent male companionship in the future. All of which serves to show how even a perfectly innocent comment about an apparently safe and unthreatening matter can unleash a flood of emotion.

A plate of jelly

Betty is a medium and a clairvoyant, and on one occasion while she was wearing her medium's hat, Betty passed on the message to a lady client about a children's birthday party, in which a naughty lad of about five years old was throwing a plate of jelly at a little girl of about the same age. Before Betty could ask her client whether she understood the message, the poor woman burst into tears. It turned out that the lady's husband had died several months previously, and she had come to see Betty with the intention of getting in touch with her late hubby in order to see if he was all right. It turned out that the birthday party in question was the occasion at which the client and her husband had first met. He had been the naughty little boy who threw the jelly and she had been the little girl who had got a face full of it.

This was obviously clear evidence that the lady's husband was keen to contact and assure her that it was him she was speaking to.

Can I have all the good stuff now please?

Timing of events is tricky. Astrologers and numerologists have more luck with this than other types of readers, but it still can work out differently from what we see. The spirit world does not understand time in the way that we do, so it can throw all kinds of chronological spanners in the works. Human nature wants all the good stuff to happen *now* and unfortunately, the laws of karma often mean having to live through a fair amount of crap before the good stuff arrives - if it ever does!

Things are rarely wonderful in every direction at once, and if a client's love life is going well, you can be sure that his business is in trouble or that his health is letting him down. Life is rarely what the clients want it to be and they sometimes take this disappointment out on us rather than railing at the gods or at themselves - either of whom may be responsible for their condition. Many clients have an agenda of what they want to hear, (that they will soon meet their soul mate, that they will be rich and famous, and so on). Others need you to guarantee them a totally ridiculous future lifestyle.

The invention of the British national lottery is something else that most Readers could do without, as there are any number of clients who genuinely hope that you will tell them exactly when they will win this mythical pile of Midas gold. Some are certain that we have the ability to furnish them with the winning numbers. As there is a fourteen million to one chance of anyone winning the lottery, I guess that if a Reader were to see fourteen million clients, one of these might turn out to be a lottery winner!

Proof of the pudding, or, did I say that?

It is very sad to see a client who has his or her heart set on someone who clearly doesn't reciprocate their feelings. It is even worse when one realises that a client is being led up the garden path, both by the other person and also by his or her own expectations. The

---

Sasha's stories...

Many years ago I was visited by a female client whom I shall call Cynthia. Cynthia was an attractive divorcee in her early forties who had been seduced by her boss. This man had showered her with presents and compliments before and into the early days of the affair, cleverly holding out the carrot she most wanted - that of marriage and respectability. Once the affair got further under way and she became hooked on his promises - and also somewhat in love with him - her boss naturally procrastinated about divorcing his wife, etc. etc. The present-giving only resumed whenever Cynthia threatened to leave her job and to end the affair. Cynthia was understandably upset by all this but she was still hopeful, still wanting to believe the fairy tales that this man spun.

Some months after the reading, Cynthia phoned and told me that she was very upset with me. Apparently I had assured her that she would be living in matrimonial harmony with her boss later that year and (according to Cynthia), I had definitely said that the situation would be quite different by the following November. Despite my apparent prophecy, this event had not occurred and indeed her boss had finally pushed the increasingly demanding and miserable Cynthia out of his office and out of his life.

> I remembered that this had been an astrological reading and I also knew that I had taped the reading, so I asked Cynthia to visit me, bringing the tape with her. We listened to it together. My voice on the tape clearly said that there would be a turning point in November and from that point onwards, Cynthia would know where all this was leading, for good or for ill. The poor woman had clearly put her own interpretation on the reading, and as she sat and listened to the tape with me, she saw what she had done. I guess that after this event Cynthia began to accept that the affair was truly over and that she must move on with her life.

following story illustrates both this syndrome and also a way of correcting a client's false assumptions.

What can and cannot be expected from a reading

Don't forget that we are not gods or goddesses, and we only see shadows. Experienced Readers and their clients will tell of many readings that were just that bit off-centre and where the situation has been spotted but slightly wrongly interpreted. Oddly enough, your clients will often be intrigued by the way things work out.

I have had many clients who have come back to me after a year or two and told me that the things I said did happen, but not in quite the way that they thought or in the way that I said they would. This is a common situation and one that the vast majority of clients take in their stride, except of course for the occasional dastardly type who may try to rip-off the Reader for being anything less than perfect.

Over-demanding clients

Nowadays clients are quite open about visiting a Reader and they will happily tell their friends and colleagues all about their visit, both before and afterwards. In days gone by, it was a different story and many clients kept quiet about such activities, because they didn't want to be thought crazy. This meant that a Reader couldn't cancel an appointment once it had been made. The chickens caused by this problem came to roost occasionally when, by the time of the appointment, the Reader was ill.

Sasha's stories...

On one occasion many years ago, I was sick with the flu and stupid enough to let a demanding client in. I was probably too ill to stand up for myself and to get rid of her. Naturally the client wasn't going to be satisfied with a quick Tarot reading, she needed a full astrological job done. I worked my way through the task of making up the chart (by hand in those days) and of interpreting her character and all the other details that arose.

Eventually I guess I struck upon the problem that was bothering her. This lady was a junior nurse of some kind who had taken a polite comment or two that had been made in passing by a senior doctor to be a declaration of undying love and a definite proposal of marriage. The client's fixed and demanding mental attitude had determined the way things were going to be, and her gold-plated vision of the future included a large house in the country, complete with upper-class children and a Labrador or two. She couldn't understand why her vision was not actually turning into reality, and she was not interested in any doubts as to the outcome of her scenario.

If a client arrives on the doorstep to find a Reader down with the flu, he or she is usually understanding enough to go away and arrange to phone for another appointment at a later date. However, some are insistent that they have their reading, despite the fact that the poor Reader has clearly just got out of bed to answer the door.

Even this story is not as bad as that of a friend of mine whom I shall call Lorraine, who had to spend some time in hospital getting over a nasty operation on her leg. Once the other patients on the ward realised that Lorraine was a healer, they pestered her to work her healing magic on them and the silly girl gave in to their demands to her own detriment.

All of which goes to show that running a consultancy is far from being a way of earning money for old rope, and that it takes knowledge, patience, wit and stamina. The best relief for those times when the clients drive you mad is to have a few pals in the same line, so that you can get together, off-load your horror stories on to each other and have a good laugh about them at the same time.

Sasha's stories...

The Royal Marine Bandsman syndrome

At long last you get to find out what the intriguing reference on the back of this book is all about.

I once was consulted by a client whom I shall call Kathy. Kathy was having an affair with a Royal Marine Bandsman, and the affair was heading for the end of the road. Kathy was understandably unhappy about this. While reading Kathy's cards, something strange kept nudging me and I felt that her desperation about all this had less to do with losing the man himself but that it had something to do with his job. This was so weird that I questioned Kathy about it, and she told me that she herself had a deep seated desire to be a Royal Marine Bandsman! The fact that she was female, only five feet four in height, fifty-one years of age and that she could neither march nor play an instrument, were definite drawbacks to this strange desire.

Kathy had felt that the only way that she felt that she could come close to meeting this need was by sleeping with someone who actually was what she so badly wanted to be! No wonder Kathy was distraught at the thought of losing her lover.

While Kathy was pouring this sad story out to me, I kept having visions of the kind of person who is so paranoid that he thinks he is Napoleon Buonaparte - you know the one I mean - the man who walks around all day with his hand tucked inside his jacket. I didn't know what to say to Kathy except to suggest that she seek out another current or an ex Royal Marine Bandsman to replace the one she had lost.

Nowadays, having accumulated more knowledge and experience than I had then, I would explain to Kathy the power of past lives and suggest that she find a good regression therapist to dig up what seems to me to be an obvious past-life connection. Perhaps this would have helped Kathy to remove the strange spell that she (an otherwise sensible and humorous woman) seemed to be living under.

Chapter 25

PROFILES OF A FEW READERS

Jonathan Dee – Roy Gillett – Sue Lilly – Sheila McGuirk – Tracey Risman – Dave & Eve Bingham – Molly-Ann Fairley – Betty Nugent

What makes anyone become a Reader? Surely no youngster decides upon this as a career option? Could you imagine the conversation between a teenager and his or her school career advisor if they asked for help to become a Rune or Tarot Reader? Well, we all got into this business somehow, so if you would like to compare your own introduction to our fascinating world with the experiences of others, let us introduce you to a cross-section of professional Readers. All the Readers mentioned below have given us valuable advice that appears in various parts of this book. We hope that this not only enlivens the book but that it shows you how to overcome problems that you yourself might meet on your journey towards your own successful consultancy.

Jonathan Dee

Jonathan and I met through my being asked to be a guest on a radio programme called Star Check that Jonathan was presenting in the late 1980s for BBC Radio Wales. Since then we have become firm friends, we have collaborated in the production of five sets of annual Astro-guides, and we have helped each other research and write countless other books. We have done numerous radio and television programmes together and we speak to each other on the phone almost daily. It is odd that the two men in my life - my husband, Jan Budkowski, and my friend and work mate, Jon Dee - both met me "on air" and only later in the flesh, so to speak.

Jon comes from a truly psychic family, as two of his grandmothers were Spiritual mediums and his father had once had psychic training. However, as Jon's dad died when Jon was only eleven years old it was years later that he discovered all this. On his mother's side, his Granny was a Spiritual medium and his mother - although not involved in the business in any way - is also a natural psychic.

Jonathan himself trained in a Spiritualist development circle but he found that this was not for him, so he turned increasingly to the Tarot and astrology. He tells me that he finds the structure of astrology easier to work with than the use of psychism alone. Jon and I are of the same mind as I also prefer to work with a client's chart, at least in the first instance. A typically witty Jon-type remark is that he "finds the dead, dead boring!"

Jonathan says that he became a professional astrologer by pure accident - or by fate if you prefer to look at it that way. Jon found himself flat broke, out of work and out of luck, so he turned towards giving readings as a way to ease himself out of debt. He discovered that he was very good at the job and that he could earn far more money by doing so than by any of the other means at his disposal at that time. By chance, four months into his temporary career as an astrologer, Jonathan found himself doing a chart for someone who worked at BBC Radio Wales. The radio station needed a regular astrologer and now - fifteen years later - he is still there, doing daily horoscopes for the BBC in Wales.

Jon and I have had parallel careers as we have both done "the lot", so to speak. We have both worked for newspapers and magazines, we have produced prerecorded phone lines, we have both travelled and worked in other countries and we have both taught, lectured and written about esoteric subjects at all kinds of levels.

Jonathan has another string to his bow as he is also known as a historian. Jon has had books published on history, mythology and prophecies, and he also broadcasts on historical subjects. Oddly enough, I also have a deep interest in history, albeit different periods of history from those that Jonathan has studied. We are both

Gemini rising and the remainder of our horoscopes are extremely similar. We may not be brother and sister in real life but spiritually, that is just what we are.

Roy Gillett

Feeling that astrology offered very valuable insights into individual and social behaviour that was being unfortunately neglected by society at large, Roy left a senior school teaching post in 1976 to devote himself full time to astrology. He has given thousands of consultations, organised many conferences and he wrote astrology descriptions of each day between 1978 and 1990. More recently, Roy has been British distributor of an advanced range of general and research astrology software. He has also been engaged in research into financial astrology, and has for some time now held senior positions in the Astrological Association of Great Britain.

Sue Lilly

Sue is a professional astrologer and she is also a health therapist. Sue said that her interest in astrology came about while she was training to be a yoga teacher in the late 1970s. During one of the training sessions, the students were asked to talk about some of their interests. It so happened that a number of them were involved with the White Eagle Lodge where these students had learned astrology. Sue's interest was sparked, but even more so when she had a chart and report done for herself. Sue said that this "blew her mind" to such an extent that she had to put it aside and allow the shock of having her nature exposed on paper to subside somewhat before she could take the report out again and give it some thought.

A little later, Sue herself took the White Eagle Lodge's astrology course and she began to give readings to friends. As her confidence and her reputation grew, Sue found herself earning some much needed money from this venture. During the mid 1990s, Sue managed the postal astrology course for the British Astrological and Psychic Society. Sue still gives readings and also works as a healer and therapist in the south west of England. Sue's husband, Simon, is also deeply involved in the esoteric field and he gives Rune readings.

Sue was responsible for much of the detailed information on taxation for self-employed readers and therapists that appears in the tax and record keeping chapter of this book.

Sheila McGuirk

Sheila is a skilled "scientific palmist". The term scientific palmist or scientific handreader, differentiates from those who take a client's hand in order to tune in on a clairvoyant level. As it happens Sheila is also a clairvoyant, so she can bring together her psychism and intuition along with her deep knowledge of the hand to give an exceptional quality of reading. Sheila specialises in health problems but she is extremely skilled in all the topics that are likely to come up during a reading.

Sheila said that she had a profound psychic experience at an early age when she looked into her bedroom mirror and saw a woman standing behind her. When Sheila turned around there was nobody there, but when she turned back to the mirror, sure enough this oddly familiar looking vision shimmered in the reflection.

Sheila ran to tell her grandmother of the experience, and this wise woman pointed out to Sheila that the vision was a kindly one as it was merely a visitation from her deceased mother who wanted to wish her beloved daughter well. Sheila's grandmother was, of course, a psychic herself and it was through this family connection that Sheila became drawn into Spiritualism. She later became fascinated by hand reading and she taught herself this subject to a very high standard.

Sheila's advice, which is repeated in the relevant section of this book, is for new Readers to do all they can to gain experience and to increase their confidence. Sheila commented that as her three children worked their way through the local schools, she became a regular feature at all their school fetes, reading hands for a small fee and increasing her confidence as each of these occasions came and went.

However, it was Sheila's first comment to us that is the most thought provoking; it was that she didn't think it was actually possible to make a living out of being a Reader. In her opinion, this is an excellent way to top up some other form of income, but it is not possible to make a living by giving readings alone, far less it is possible to support a family by this business. Naturally there are Readers who would agree and Readers who would disagree with Sheila, so it is up to the individual to decide for him or herself.

Tracey Risman

Tracey is our beginner and we have been watching her progress with great interest throughout the time that we have been compiling the information for this book. Tracey, who is our niece, (more accurately, Sasha's niece), is in her early 30s. Tracey started working in the esoteric field about two years ago when she took a job at a dial-a-psychic phone-line company. The company offered her training in Tarot and clairvoyance before letting her loose on the phones. We are all extremely impressed with the quality of the training at the centre where Tracey worked and it certainly brought out all Tracey's latent psychic and mediumistic abilities.

It is not surprising that someone in the family would take up this kind of work, as the family has been dotted with psychic and spiritual personalities throughout the generations. Unfortunately the Tarot phone-line centre folded, but it left Tracey with an urge to pursue her mystical career further. She has taken lessons in astrology from Aunty Sasha and she is now busy learning how to read hands. She is not sure which branch will be her ultimate one because at the moment, she is exploring all three and giving professional readings at the same time.

Sasha is not a bit surprised that Tracey should be the one to take up the family business, having watched Tracey work in one "caring and helping" field after another. Sasha's own offspring are knowledgeable about esoteric matters, and fortunately their spouses are also extremely intuitive and very accepting of our strange family profession, but it is Tracey who is set to carry the torch into the future. Like Sasha and Jonathan, Tracey has Gemini rising, which is the zodiac sign of the writer and broadcaster, so look out for her first book on the Tarot later this year.

It is Tracey's struggles to get her fledgling business off the ground that have inspired some of the ideas in this book.

Dave and Eve Bingham

Dave Bingham said that he would never have become a medium and healer if it hadn't been raining!

Dave's mother liked to visit her local Spiritualist Church to see the mediums at work and to have a bit of healing when she felt the need for it, and it was Dave who was often dragooned into giving her a lift to and from her Church. On this particular evening, the traffic was heavy and the rain was coming down, as Dave says "in stair-rods", so instead of trailing back home and then having to turn around and come back to fetch his mother again, Dave invested a "half-crown" and went in. That did it. Dave then became trained as a platform medium and later on, with his wife, Eve, they became Readers and healers in their turn, with Dave specialising in the ancient Egyptian geomantic art of sand reading. He also reads Tarot, the crystal ball and anything else that he can use in order to create a psychic link.

Dave's and Eve have worked together and separately as Mediums, clairvoyants, Tarot and crystal Readers for many years. At some points in their lives, they have been able to rely on readings for a living and at others they have used their skills as top-up income. In my opinion, the most exciting thing that Dave and Eve have done is to run the wonderful Earth Spirit festivals in the Watershed, Bristol, Malvern winter gardens and many other venues throughout the country.

Another way they work that until this time has not been documented, is the Specialised Healing that both Dave and Eve carry out to bring back into balance and harmony both the physical and Spiritual alignment within people and dwellings. They look at this as a healing process rather than exorcism, or what is commonly known as "Ghost Busting".

This service they perform in a kind, quiet, gentle manner, for in most cases it is found that families with small children are involved. They do not advertise this service, as usually people that have such problems tend to find their way to Dave and Eve. These clearings do not have a set format, as each case has specialised needs.

There was a spate a few years ago, when quite a number of well-known mediums needed their services to help clear their own spiritual channels and balance their energies.

As you can imagine, these types of workings should only be carried out by those with years of knowledge, experience and understanding of the forces of nature, Earth Energies and the Power of Spirit, so a beginner should not try these as a starting point.

Dave and Eve also maintain that it is impossible to rely totally upon giving Readings as a living, but that it is a useful source of top-up income. They also maintain that working in a "proper job" helps a Reader to keep some perspective and to understand the pressures that their clients are facing in their everyday lives. Their interests give them something to go out for, and a chance to meet others and to make new friends. Dave and Eve both give readings, teach esoteric subjects and they give healing and spiritual advice to anybody who needs it.

Molly-Ann Fairley

It is hard to pigeonhole Molly-Ann as she doesn't really fit into a category, although she terms herself a healer. We suppose that the best description would be that Molly-Ann is first and foremost a person who heals those who are sick in mind and spirit. Molly-Ann is also a psychic, a medium and a Tarot Reader, and an excellent teacher and communicator. However, it is her unique combination of techniques, coupled with her work on the etheric level that is so magical. Molly-Ann identifies blockages within her clients and then removes them. This is regardless of whether the blockage is in the here and now of their conscious or subconscious mind, or whether it is something that is buried within their past. The same goes for whether the problem comes from a past life experience or even an unwarranted attack from a spiritual entity. So, now let Molly-Ann describe some of her work in her own words.

Molly-Ann's views

In my case, I have seen over the past twelve years of private practice that, even if the client has insisted that there was no conscious reason for their particular problem, there has always been one. There is no effect without cause, be it health problems, financial problems, too much weight, unhappiness, depression, failure, lack of confidence or learning difficulties - it doesn't matter what. If this is really so, and if the cause can be traced and accessed from the subconscious mind and deep physical cellular structure in the body or even from an unworldly cause, what a fabulous opportunity we all have for the possibility of a cure. I see miracles of this nature every single day!

Betty Nugent

Betty Nugent has been a medium, clairvoyant, sand, crystal and Tarot Reader for the past 34 years. Betty is a widow and she is also our oldest Reader; she is happy for us to tell you that she is 75 years old, and she is still working at full stretch! Why? Betty says that she cannot live in anything other than a hand-to-mouth manner on the British old-age pension and she isn't content to live in such a manner.

Thus Betty is prepared to keep working for as long as she can, in order to keep her car on the road and to live comfortably. She doesn't ever see herself giving up work. Betty told us that she and others like her find it difficult to get enough business through the door at her home, so she goes out to psychic festivals and to group or party-plan reading sessions that are arranged by her many contacts throughout the country.

Betty told us that many years ago, an aunt had taken her to see a trance medium, and she was somewhat amazed by this strange woman who spoke to them in a "funny voice". Much later a friend invited Betty to an evening of clairvoyance at a local Spiritualist

Church and, somewhat over the objections of her martinet of a husband, Betty insisted in going along.

After that, Betty never missed a service, meeting or a session in the development circle, and this eventually led to the career that is happily carrying her through her sunshine years! Betty has contributed some wonderfully useful tips for this book and her wise words will turn up here and there throughout this work.

WHEN IT ALL GOES RIGHT!

In this closing chapter, Jan and I have unashamedly repeated a section from the introduction in order to make our point.

The benefits of running a consultancy

The benefits of running a Reader's consultancy are many and varied. A consultancy offers self-employment to those who have had enough of working for an employer, a bridge while looking for a new job, a replacement income for those who have been made redundant, or a creative outlet for mothers of small children who can only devote a couple of hours a week to the task. It can suit those who need to work from home, and those who want to travel the world and earn money while on the move.

There is a "feel-good" factor in helping others and in giving a good service to those who need it, and there is also an inner satisfaction to be derived from working in a spiritual manner. Our work has room for those who are mystical, practical, artistic, down-to-earth, academic, earthy, ordinary and extraordinary. There is room for every type of Reader in every discipline, and there are clients with a plethora of different needs out there to be taken care of.

Our epilogue

At the end of the day, becoming a Reader is not a choice that is lightly taken. It is not the kind of career that a schoolchild sees him or herself taking up. It is in the nature of a vocation, possibly something that you are driven into. All the ups and downs, the hazards of self-employment and the difficulties of the job, are compensated for by its subtle benefits. The path that Jan and I have taken is also a spiritual one in its way, because we gather together information in order to produce books of all levels in the mind, body and spirit field, in order to help those of you who are seeking knowledge and understanding to find them.

May the force be with us all!

Sasha and Jan, May 1999

APPENDIX

Useful Resources

Please note: There are some dialling code changes due in the UK in mid-1999, but we understand that the old codes will remain in use for another year or so. There will obviously be changes in addresses and telephone numbers anyway, as time goes on, and this is the unfortunate part of putting addresses into a book. Partly for this reason, we are limiting the number of addresses included here. You will find a much more comprehensive and up-to-date list on our website (www.zampub.com). The website will have lots of other information available, as well as details of current and forthcoming Zambezi books. Our catch-phrase for Zambezi is "more than just books...", and we intend to maintain a range of interesting content available to you on our website. We've only just registered the web name and Jan has the job of creating the site, but by the time you read this, our site should be up and running (i.e. by early June 1999). Visit us on the site!

Amazon on-line bookshop

www.amazon.com (USA)
www.amazon.co.uk (UK & Europe)

American Federation of Astrologers, Inc.

P.O. Box 22040
Tempe
AZ 85285-2040
USA
Tel: +1 (888) 301 7630
e-mail: AFA@msn.com

Association for Astrological Networking (AFAN)

8306 Wilshire Boulevard
Suite 537
Beverley Hills
CA 90211
USA

Astro Originals (Arielle Guttman)

(excellent astrological courses, seminars, tapes, books)
P.O. Box 15006
Santa Fe
New Mexico
NM 87506
USA
Tel: +1 505 984 8330
Fax: +1 505 984 0048
e-mail: info@arielle.com
web: www.arielle.com

Astrolabe USA

(Solar Fire range of astrological software)
P.O. Box 1750
Brewster
MA 02631
Tel: +1 508 896 5081
Fax: +1 508 896 5289
e-mail: astrolabe@alabe.com
web: www.alabe.com

Astrological Association of Great Britain

Unit 168,
Lee Valley Technopark
Tottenham
Hale,
London N17 9LN
Tel: +44 (0)181 880 4848

Fax: +44 (0)181 880 4849
e-mail:
web: www.astrologer.com/aanet/index.html

Astrological Institute of Research and Study (AIRS)

P.O. Box 10235
Rivonia 2128
Gauteng,
South Africa
Tel: +27 (0)11 807 1791
Fax: +27 (0)11 807 1071

Astrological Lodge of London

50 Gloucester Place
London W1H 4EA
UK

Astrological Society of South Africa

P.O. Box 481
Cresta 2118
Gauteng
RSA
Tel: +27 (0)11 867 4153

Astrology Shop, The

(if the book exists, they will either have it or find it.)
78 Neal Street
Covent Garden
London WC2H 9PA
Tel: +44 (0)171 497 1001
Fax: +44 (0)171 497 0344
e-mail: equinox@equinox.uk.com
web: www.astrology.co.uk

Astrolore

(Astrology magazine)

P.O. Box 3339
Poole
Dorset BH12 4ZE
UK
Tel: +44 (0)1202 73 5601
e-mail: marketing@astrolore.demon.co.uk
web: www.astrolore.demon.co.uk

Bertelsmann's on-line bookshop
www.bol.com

Blackwell's on-line bookshop
www.blackwell.co.uk

British Astrological and Psychic Society (BAPS)
Robert Denholme House
Bletchingley Road
Nutfield
Surrey RH1 4HW
UK
Tel/Fax: +44 (0)7071 78 0796
e-mail: baps@tlpplc.com
web: www.bapsoc.co.uk

Bookspeed
(Book distributors)
62 Hamilton Place
Edinburgh EH3 5AZ
Scotland
Tel: +44 (0)131 225 4950
Fax: +44 (0)131 220 6515
e-mail: sales@bkspeed.demon.co.uk

Budkowski, Jan
see Zambezi Publishing

California Institute of Integral Studies
   (astrological studies)
   765 Ashbury Street
   San Francisco
   CA 94117
   USA
   Tel: +1 415 753 6100

Centre for Psychological Astrology
   (astrological seminars)
   BCM Box 1815
   London WC1N 3XX
   Tel/Fax: +44 (0)181 749 2330

Dee, Jonathan
   e-mail: jondee@zampub.com

Esoteric Technologies (Pty) Ltd.
   (Solar Fire astrological software)
   P.O. Box 159
   Stepney
   SA 5069
   South Australia
   Tel/Fax: +61 8 331 3057

Faculty of Astrological Studies
   54 High Street
   Orpington
   Kent BR6 0JQ
   UK
   Tel: +44 (0)7000 79 0143
   Fax: +44 (0)1689 60 3537
   e-mail: info@astrology.org.uk
   web: www.astrology.org.uk

Fairley, Molley Ann
Kingston School of Psychic Studies

20 Blenheim Gardens
Kingston
Surrey KT2 7BW
UK
Tel: +44 0181 974 6792
e-mail: molly@zampub.com

Federation of Australian Astrologers

P.O. Box 159
Stepney
SA 5069
South Australia
Tel/Fax: +61 8 331 3057

Fenton, Sasha

see Zambezi Publishing

Helpline for:

Contributions Agency (National Insurance),
Inland Revenue,
Customs & Excise (VAT)
(UK)
Tel: 0345 143 143

Gillett, Roy B. Ed (Hons Ldn) ACII
Roy Gillett Consultants,

32 Glynswood,
Camberley,
Surrey GU15 1HU
UK
Tel / Fax: +44 (0)1276 68 3898;
e-mail: roy.gillett@dial.pipex.com;
Distributes Astrolabe astrology software, including the leading
Solar Fire range for general astrology, astro-mapping, research and

interpretation report generation. Roy also offers personal research advice, especially in the area of business personnel and financial projection.

Horoscope magazine
Allen House
East Borough
Wimbourne
Dorset BH21 1PF
UK
Tel: +44 (0)1202 88 1749
Fax: +44 (0)1202 84 1692

Lilly, Sue
Sue's work is divided into two main areas of activity. One area covers her role as a complementary practitioner (Health Kinesiology and Nutrition) and astrologer, the other, within Mandragora Complementary Studies, as a lecturer, specialising in flower essences and plant spirit medicine.
Exeter, Devon,
UK
Tel: +44 (0)1392 83 2005
e-mail: sue@greenmantrees.demon.co.uk

Howard S. Markham and Company
(Chartered accountants)
10 Perrins Lane
Hampstead NW3 1QY
UK
Tel: 0171 794 0171
Fax: 0171 431 1910
(Howard is our accountant, we're very satisfied with his company's services, and he is perfectly happy to take on Readers as clients. He doesn't poke fun at our type of work.)

Matrix UK

(Winstar astrological software)
c/o Martin Davis
Library wing
Abbey St. Bathan's House
Duns,
Berwickshire TD11 3TX
Scotland
Tel: +44 (0)1361 84 0340
Fax: +44 (0)1361 84 0284
e-mail: martin@astral.demon.co.uk

Matrix USA

(Bluestar / Winstar astrological software)
315 Marion Avenue
Big Rapids
MI 49307
USA
Tel: +1 616 796 2483
Fax: +1 616 796 3060
web: http://thenewage.com

Merlin's Cave

(MB&S books)
Wales
web: http://members.aol.com/esoporium

MicroCycles, Inc.

(astrological software - all sorts)
P.O. Box 3175
Culver City
CA 90231
USA
Tel: +1 310 202 8337
Fax: +1 310 202 6365

Mountain Astrologer, The

(Astrological magazine)
P.O. Box 970
Cedar Ridge
CA 95924
USA
Tel: +1 800 948 8048
Fax: +1 530 477 7756
e-mail: Ads@MountainAstrologer.com
web: www.MountainAstrologer.com

Mysteries

(MB&S shop - it has practically everything...)
9-11 Monmouth Street
Covent Garden
London WC2H 9DA
UK
Tel: +44 (0)171 240 3688

Para Publishing

P.O. Box 8206-240
Santa Barbara,
CA 93118-8206
USA
Tel: +1 805 968 7277
Fax: +1 805 968-1379
e-mail: DanPoynter@parapublishing.com
info@parapublishing.com
web: www.parapublishing.com

Prediction magazine

(MB&S magazine)
Tel: +44 (0)181 686 2599
e-mail: prediction@lhm.co.uk

Psychic News
(MB&S journal)
Tel: +44 (0)1279 81 7050

Publishers Marketing Association
627 Aviation Way
Manhattan Beach
CA 90266
USA
Tel: +1 (310) 372 2732
Fax: +1 (310) 374 3342
e-mail: info@pma-online.org
web: pma-online.org

Southern Cross Academy
(astrology)
71 Buckingham Avenue
Craighall Park 2196
Gauteng,
South Africa
Tel: +27 (0)11 447 1055

Thorburn School of Astrology
P.O. Box 146288
Bracken Gardens 1452
Gauteng,
South Africa
Tel: +27 (0)11 867 4153

Ulysees
(Astrological bookshop)
23 4th Avenue
Parkhurst
Johannesburg
South Africa
Tel: +27 (0)11 447 5958

Fax: +27 (0)11 447 5859

Urania Trust, The
396 Caledonian Road
London N1 1DN
Tel: +44 (0)171 700 0639
Fax: +44 (0)171 700 6479
e-mail: urania@globalnet.co.uk

Waterstone's on-line bookshop
Web: www.waterstone.co.uk

Watkins books
(MB&S specialists, also Tarot cards)
21 Cecil Court
Charing Cross Road
London W2 4EZ
Tel: +44 (0)171 836 2182
Fax: +44 (0)171 836 3778
e-mail: service@watkinsbooks.com
Web: www.watkinsbooks.com

Zambezi Publishing
(also Sasha & Jan's contact address)
P.O. Box 188
Brentford
Middlesex TW8 8RW
UK
Fax: +44 (0)181 568-4992
e-mail: zambezi@compuserve.com
         info@zampub.com
         sasha@zampub.com
         jan@zampub.com
web: www.zampub.com

Index

F

Faculty of Astrologers 114

Fairley, Molly-Ann 135, 214

fairs 48

Fairs and Festivals 70

Family friction 37

Federation of Spiritual Healers 12

fee structure 87

fees 65

Feng Shui 35, 63, 136, 164

Fenton, Sasha 89, 102

Festival of Mind, Body and Spirit 99

Fiddles 172

Files and filing 143

Financial uncertainty 127

fluctuating income 127

fonts 141

Food and drink 30

Foreign clients 197

formula 92

fortune-teller 98

Fraudulent mediums 98

Freeware 79

friend's home 45

fund-raising fairs 70

G

garden party 185

Gillett, Roy 210

graphologists 52, 63

graphology 50, 53, 78, 94

Groups 14

H

hand prints 77

healers 59

Zambezi Publishing
More than just books...

Have you read:

ASTROLOGY ON THE MOVE!

"Where on Earth should you be?"

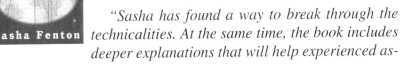

- In her inimitable, easy-to-read style, Sasha explains how a change of location may have the answer to your work, health or romantic problems.
- You don't have to be an astrologer to use and understand geographic astrology. Few other books exist on this subject, none make it as accessible as this one does.

"Sasha has found a way to break through the technicalities. At the same time, the book includes deeper explanations that will help experienced astrologers."
Roy Gillett, Chair, Astrological Association of Great Britain.

"A person with very little working knowledge of astrology would be able to get a lot out of this book... A thorough grasp of this subject brought clearly to life."
Colin Wareham, Astrolore magazine

Paperback, ISBN 0-9533478-0-X   £10.95

Your Millennium Forecast Book

by
Sasha Fenton & Jonathan Dee

Here is all the information you need
to predict your future trends, in one terrific package!
All twelve signs are covered in this book!

If you enjoy reading your stars for entertaining and informative advice on your future, you will find this book a real feast!

Jonathan and Sasha offer you readings for the year 2000 and for the first decade of the new millennium. These are followed by an overview of each month and a reading for each and every week of the year 2000, showing the major planetary movements that will influence you throughout the year.

Jonathan and Sasha describe your character by using both western and Chinese astrology, then set out clearly what you can expect during the year of the Dragon.

New compatibility charts show you with whom you will get on best as a friend or lover in the new year.

Paperback, ISBN 0-9533478-2-   (about £8.00)
"Your Millennium Forecast Book" will be available
from October 1999... (perhaps sooner!)
*Send in the mailing list application form at the back of this book
if you wish to be advised as soon as the book is published.*

LOOKING TO THE FUTURE

The revised version of Prophecy for Profit

If there is anything that you think we have left out in this current book or if you have any tips that would be useful to other Readers, please let us know and we will include them when we produce revised versions. We will list your name in the acknowledgement section if you wish us to do so.

An Alternative Income

We intend to produce a book that we are calling An Alternative Income, which will be aimed at those who work in a variety of self-employed careers of a healing nature. We wish to provide information for those who work in the fields of alternative and complementary therapies, treatments, medicine, healing and so forth. We hope that the new book will also be useful for those who work as beauticians, counsellors or in any career that offers a helpful service to the public on a personal basis. If you work in these fields and if you have any information that you would like us to pass on to others via our next book, you might like to answer some of the questions in our questionnaire.

Questionnaire

We have compiled this brief questionnaire, and if you feel like photocopying the pages and sending your thoughts to us (or e-mailing the information to us), we will look at them and hopefully include them. If you like, we can list your name in the acknowledgements section of the book. If you wish to stay anonymous, we will respect your choice.

Personal details

You don't have to give us your name or any other personal details at all, but if you wish to do so for publication, and if we use your information, your name will appear in the acknowledgement list.

Your name:
Your disciplines (e.g. aromatherapist etc.):
The number of years you have been working in this field:

Skills and qualifications
We understand that since January 1992, under EU regulations, all those who advertise treatments must be registered. Could you tell us what qualifications are available in your particular line and also which is the registering body (and their address) in your country.

Counselling skills
In your opinion, does a therapist also need to be a counsellor? If so should they take some specific training for this? Are there specific training courses, from which body, and what is their address?

Location
Is it possible to do your kind of work from home, and if not, what other venues would be suitable? This includes temporary arrangements or work at health festivals, etc.

Staff and organisational methods
Does your kind of work require a receptionist, bookkeeper or other staff? Can this easily be shared with other practitioners? Is there anything that is not already covered in "Prophecy for Profit" regarding the running of a practice that you feel we should be including?

Start-up and running costs
Where does the money go? The costs involved in rent, kitting out a room at home, special equipment and facilities, cleaning costs, etc. We don't necessarily need to know your specific figures for these, although this would be useful information to beginners, but

even an idea of the kind of items that cost money at the outset and typical costs that increase as the business progresses grows would be useful.

Tax and legal matters

Is there anything about taxation or indeed any other legal or official matter (for your country) that you think should be included? If you have any information of this kind, please could you mention which country you are operating in, as things will differ from one place to another.

Building a clientele

The advice for this will be different for therapists compared to astrologers, etc. Have you any tips that we can pass on? For example, is it a good idea to have a board outside the premises to advertise what is on offer? What kind of advertising do you find to be most effective?

Charges

Is there anything that you think should be added in a book about therapists regarding finding the right price for your work? On what basis do you decide your charging structure?

Combining jobs

Is it possible to combine your work with allied jobs such as teaching and writing? Is it possible to do your work on a part-time basis, perhaps with another part-time job that brings in a regular income?

The media

Do you find it worth doing television or anything similar - either as part of an income or for promotional purposes?

Stress

The work of a therapist may be more physical than that of a Tarot Reader, but mental as well as physical stress levels will still exist. Is there anything you can recommend as a stress-buster? Writers and publishers also suffer from stress, so any advice would be useful!

Finally,

Think about any issues that "Prophecy for Profit" may not cover regarding your discipline(s). Your comments about any such issues, and any tips about how to deal with them, would be useful.

Sasha and I hope that you enjoyed reading this book,
that you gained some knowledge from it,
and that you'll put what you learned to good use.

Zambezi Publishing is a relatively new "child" of ours,
and we plan to release a growing number of books
in the foreseeable future.
The subject matter will remain
mainly in the Mind, Body & Spirit arena,
but we intend to widen our scope
to include works by authors,
knowledgeable in their particular disciplines,
who have a worthwhile contribution to make,
and fresh insights as we enter the new Millennium.

Should you wish to be kept informed about
forthcoming titles from Zambezi Publishing,
please complete the mailing list form
within the next few pages, and fax, snail-mail,
or e-mail your details to us.
(N.B: Our mailing list will not be sold to dozens
of junk-mail distributors).

If you're interested in astrology,
you might like to read the advert about
Sasha's recently published book, "Astrology... on the Move!"
This book brings the concepts of Astro-maps and Local Space
into plain, easily digestible English.
It is also the first book on the subject
to include Chiron interpretations.

You'll also find our books on major UK Internet bookshops,
and on our own website in the foreseeable future.
Our web address is:
www.zampub.com

MAIL LIST REQUEST

Fax request: +44 (0)181 568-4992

e-mail: zambezi@compuserve.com

Postal: P.O. Box 188
Brentford,
Middlesex TW8 8RW
UK

Please add my name to your mailing list for:
(x marks the spot):
____ Notification of all future Zambezi Publishing titles;
____ Notification of specific title(s) to be released, namely:
a) _____
b) _____
No. of copies that *may* be required (not cast in stone):
a) _____ b) _____

Company name
(if applicable): _____

(block capitals, please):
Name: _____
Address: _____
_____
_____
_____
City: _____ (State): _____
Zip: _____ Country: _____

Tel: (_____) _____
Fax: (_____) _____
e-mail: _____

MAIL LIST REQUEST

Fax request: +44 (0)181 568-4992

e-mail: zambezi@compuserve.com

Postal: P.O. Box 188
Brentford,
Middlesex TW8 8RW
UK

Please add my name to your mailing list for:
(x marks the spot):
_____ Notification of all future Zambezi Publishing titles;
_____ Notification of specific title(s) to be released, namely:
a) _____
b) _____
No. of copies that *may* be required (not cast in stone):
a) _____ b) _____

Company name
(if applicable): _____

(block capitals, please):
Name: _____
Address: _____

_____
_____
_____
City: _____ (State): _____
Zip: _____ Country: _____

Tel: (_____) _____
Fax: (_____) _____
e-mail: _____

ORDER FORM

Fax orders:	+44 (0)181 568-4992
e-mail orders:	zambezi@compuserve.com
Postal orders:	Zambezi Publishing
	P.O. Box 188, Brentford,
	Middlesex TW8 8RW
	UK

Please send me the following book(s):

TITLE	PRICE	NO.	TOTAL
_____	£ _____		£ _____
_____	£ _____		£ _____
_____	£ _____		£ _____
_____	£ _____		£ _____
TOTAL:			**£** _____

Company name,
(if applicable): _____

Company order No: _____

Name *(block capitals, please):* _____

Address: _____

_____

_____

_____

City: _____ (State): _____

Zip: _____ Country: _____

Tel: _____ Fax: _____

e-mail: _____

Post & packing: £1.50 for one book, 0.50p per book thereafter.

O'seas orders: p&p + £2.50; more than one book: £1 per book.

Payment: Cheque, cash, postal orders (in UK). We will accept US$ or EURO international money orders, but prevailing exchange rates plus 5% charges (on total amount) will apply. Rather send British Sterling - or order via an Internet bookshop.

ORDER FORM

Fax orders:	+44 (0)181 568-4992
e-mail orders:	zambezi@compuserve.com
Postal orders:	Zambezi Publishing
	P.O. Box 188, Brentford,
	Middlesex TW8 8RW
	UK

Please send me the following book(s):

TITLE	PRICE	NO.	TOTAL
_____	£ _____	£ _____	
_____	£ _____	£ _____	
_____	£ _____	£ _____	
_____	£ _____	£ _____	
TOTAL:		**£ _____**	

Company name,
(if applicable): _____

Company order No: _____

Name *(block capitals, please):* _____

Address: _____

_____

_____

_____

City: _____ (State): _____

Zip: _____ Country: _____

Tel: _____ Fax: _____

e-mail: _____

Post & packing: £1.50 for one book, 0.50p per book thereafter.

O'seas orders: p&p + £2.50; more than one book: £1 per book.

Payment: Cheque, cash, postal orders (in UK). We will accept US$ or EURO international money orders, but prevailing exchange rates plus 5% charges (on total amount) will apply. Rather send British Sterling - or order via an Internet bookshop.

ORDER FORM

Fax orders:	+44 (0)181 568-4992
e-mail orders:	zambezi@compuserve.com
Postal orders:	Zambezi Publishing
	P.O. Box 188, Brentford,
	Middlesex TW8 8RW
	UK

Please send me the following book(s):

TITLE	PRICE	NO.	TOTAL
_____	£ _____		£ _____
_____	£ _____		£ _____
_____	£ _____		£ _____
_____	£ _____		£ _____
TOTAL:			**£** _____

Company name,
(if applicable): _____

Company order No: _____

Name *(block capitals, please):* _____

Address: _____

_____

_____

_____

City: _____ (State): _____

Zip: _____ Country: _____

Tel: _____ Fax: _____

e-mail: _____

Post & packing: £1.50 for one book, 0.50p per book thereafter.

O'seas orders: p&p + £2.50; more than one book: £1 per book.

Payment: Cheque, cash, postal orders (in UK). We will accept US$ or EURO international money orders, but prevailing exchange rates plus 5% charges (on total amount) will apply. Rather send British Sterling - or order via an Internet bookshop.